SKILLS FOR LAWYERS

SKILLS FOR LAWYERS

Annabel Elkington MA (Hons), Dip Law, Barrister

James Greene MA (Cantab), Solicitor

John Holtam LLB (Southampton), Solicitor

Gill Morgan LLB (Bristol), Solicitor

Gemma M Shield LLB (Hons), Solicitor

Tony Simmonds BA, MA, MCLIP

JORDANS

2003

Published by
Jordan Publishing Limited
21 St Thomas Street
Bristol BS1 6JS

British Library Cataloguing-in-Publication Data
A catalogue record for this book is available from the British Library.

ISSN 1353–6648
ISBN 0 85308 889 6

Printed in Great Britain by Hobbs The Printers Ltd of Southampton

PREFACE

Knowledge of how the internal combustion engine works and what the Highway Code states does not necessarily make a good driver. In the same way, knowledge of the law does not necessarily make a good lawyer. The practice of law requires not merely an understanding of law and procedure but also the skills necessary to utilise that knowledge effectively.

The purpose of this Resource Book is to help prospective practitioners to develop fundamental skills which will prove essential in their later careers. Those skills are as follows:

(1) writing and drafting;
(2) legal research;
(3) interviewing and advising clients;
(4) negotiation; and
(5) advocacy.

The chapters covering each of these skills are essential preparatory reading for practice of the relevant skill on the Legal Practice Course. It is hoped that they will also prove useful in later years for the trainee or qualified solicitor, both to monitor one's own development and to evaluate others, learning from their successes and their failures.

Thanks are due to authors of the constituent Parts in earlier editions for originating and developing various chapters. They are:

Part I   Rachel Hawes, Priscilla Sarton
Part II   Carol Moore, Alison Baigent, Ian Cross, Stephen Sellers, Joanne Tomlinson and Susan
            Scorey
Part III   Martin Iller, Peter Mott, Deborah Green

Needless to say, the current team of authors bears responsibility for any failings in this edition.

The origins of Part III lie in a series of Professional Development courses which The College of Law ran for the solicitors' profession for a number of years. In mounting the interviewing and negotiating courses, the College received invaluable assistance from Dr Karl Mackie (now Chief Executive of the Centre for Dispute Resolution). Similarly, the courses on advocacy benefited greatly from the advice and help of His Honour Judge Groves, Her Honour Judge Marian Norrie, His Honour Judge Nigel Fricker QC and Tony Edwards, solicitor. In addition, we would wish to express our gratitude to the many solicitors who attended the courses and contributed their know-how to them, and consequently to these chapters.

CONTENTS

PART I

WRITING AND DRAFTING

Chapter 1

WRITING AND DRAFTING

1.1 INTRODUCTION

1.1.1 A solicitor's written skills

This chapter provides an introduction to the skills required by a solicitor when writing letters, reports and memoranda, and drafting legal documents.

1.1.2 How to approach this material

The notes which follow encourage you to think about the way in which you write and draft. You should apply these principles throughout all the subjects on the Legal Practice Course, not merely in exercises designed specifically to test writing and drafting. The principles of legal drafting will be further expanded in relation to the types of legal document relevant to individual subjects. You may find, however, that some solicitors' firms have their own style guides and precedents which they require you to follow, regardless of other recommendations.

1.2 DRAFTING A LEGAL DOCUMENT

We are considering here the drafting of a document that is intended to have legal effect. It is vital to remember that the putting of words onto your paper or your computer screen is one of the later steps in the drafting process. You must be certain of what you want your document to achieve before you look for words that will achieve it.

1.2.1 Preliminary steps

The preliminary steps are:

- taking instructions from your client;

- deciding how to put those instructions into effect;

- researching the law.

Taking instructions

To begin with, you must take instructions from your client. You need to know what your client wants to accomplish, and all the background facts.

However, you cannot rely on a client's instructions being complete. He may not think of every eventuality. For example, two clients who are setting up in partnership together and instructing you to draft the partnership agreement may not think to give you instructions as to provisions about taking holidays, or for payment of interest on capital. It is part of your role as draftsperson to raise these issues, advise your client and ask for further instructions.

Equally, your client may not realise that his instructions are impossible to carry out, either practically or legally. He may instruct you to impose an obligation on a buyer of part of his land to put up a 2 metre fence along what will become the common boundary. You must realise:

- that you need further details as to what type of fence this is to be;

- that a time-limit must be imposed;

- that you need to think about compelling the neighbour not just to put up the fence but to maintain it as well;

- that a fence of that height will need planning permission and that the buyer may not be able to get the permission;

- that an obligation to erect a fence is a positive obligation, so that although your client will be able to compel the **buyer** to fulfil the obligation, there are legal difficulties in the way of enforcing the obligation against anybody who may later acquire the land.

These are all matters that you must consider and, possibly, discuss with your client and on which you might have to advise him. If you do not do this, your draft cannot be fully successful.

Deciding how to put the instructions into effect

This brings us back to the fundamental questions which underlie all legal drafting: 'What are we trying to achieve and what is the best way of achieving it?'.

You must analyse your instructions. The following two questions are worth asking yourself.

(1)   Am I restricting an existing right or am I granting a new one?
(2)   Do I wish to impose an obligation on X, or to give him a right or a permission?

Let us tie this down to a simple example.

Suppose your client owns an outbuilding which has a small yard attached. He asks you to grant a lease of the area to X, and tells you that X is not to be allowed to park more than one car in the yard. When you come to deal with the question of parking, you must decide what it is your client wants us to do, in the light of the surrounding facts. If the lease is to be only of the outbuilding, then X will have no right to enter the yard unless the lease gives him that right. So you will carry out your instructions by including in the lease the right to park one car in the yard. If the lease is to be of the outbuilding **and** the yard, then X, as tenant, will have the power to do anything in the yard he likes. So this time, in order to carry out your instructions, you will draft a covenant by X that will restrict his right to park cars.

Suppose you are drafting such a covenant. Do you think the following covenant is suitable?

The Tenant covenants to park only one car in the Yard.

The covenant appears to impose an obligation on X to park a car. However, we do not intend to force him to park a car. We only want to ensure that he never parks more than one. So we should change the wording to:

The Tenant covenants not to park more than one car in the Yard.

This process of analysing your instructions and considering how to put them into effect is essential. A well organised, clearly written document is worse than useless if it achieves the wrong result.

Researching the law

You must know the relevant law. If you do not, it is impossible for you to judge the result of your draft.

1.2.2 Beginning to structure the document

When you have decided how to achieve your client's wishes, you can begin to plan the document. This can be done by:

- listing the points that the document must make;

- grouping the points into topics and giving each topic a heading;

- deciding in what order to deal with the topics.

For example, suppose that you are drafting an agreement for the hire of a car to a company. You might group together all the points that concern restrictions on the use of the car, for example:

- car to be used only by three named drivers;

- the company to warrant that the named drivers all hold full driving licences;

- car to be used only for specified purposes.

These points could then be put under the heading '**Use of Car**'.

Similarly, under the heading '**Deposit**' you could group such points as:

- promise by the company to pay a deposit of £500;

- provision for return of the deposit in certain circumstances;

- provision for retention of the deposit.

By doing this, you are planning the clauses in your document. You will also have to decide in what order to put the clauses.

1.2.3 Deciding on the structure of a document

A basic structure

Many documents will contain the following elements:

- commencement;
- date;
- parties;
- recitals;
- operative part;
- testimonium;
- schedules;
- execution and attestation.

COMMENCEMENT, DATE AND PARTIES

A document will normally begin with a 'commencement' which describes the nature of the document, for example 'This Agreement', 'This Conveyance'. Alternatively, the document's title can simply be printed as a heading. Deeds may also use the word 'deed' in the title, for example 'This deed of Conveyance'.

A space should be left for insertion of the date when the document is completed.

The full names and addresses of the parties should be inserted. (In the case of a company, the address of its registered office should be inserted.) For example:

SERVICE AGREEMENT

DATE:

PARTIES: **(1)** **Weyford Products Limited whose registered office is at 32 Bridge House, Wharf Road, Milton, Berefordshire.**

(2) **Joan Alice Bennet of 8 High Street, Milton, Berefordshire.**

A long and complicated document can benefit from an index or table of clauses (preferably at the front).

RECITALS

Recitals clauses are not essential and you should consider carefully whether or not to include them. You can use them to set out the background facts to the document and so make it more self-explanatory. For example, in a conveyance of land by a personal representative the date of the deceased's death and the date on which a grant of representation was obtained could be recited.

Recitals are also sometimes used to introduce and summarise the contents of the operative part of the document but, except in complicated documents, this is generally not necessary and increases the risk of introducing ambiguities.

OPERATIVE PART

The operative part of a document is the part which creates the legal rights and obligations.

The contents of the operative part of a document depend on the nature of the document. For example, a commercial agreement will generally contain:

- conditions precedent (setting out conditions which have to be satisfied before the agreement comes into force);

- agreements (setting out the rights and obligations of the parties);

- representations and warranties (ie statements about factual and legal matters which one of the parties requires to be made to him in a legally binding way);

- 'boiler-plate' clauses (ie standard clauses inserted into all agreements of such a type and dealing with, for example, the service of notices under the agreement, or the jurisdiction for action where the agreement has an international element).

TESTIMONIUM

A testimonium clause is not essential but, if used, it introduces the signatures of the parties and may describe a particular method of executing where, for example, a company is using its seal as part of its execution, or an attorney is signing on behalf of a party.

SCHEDULES

Use schedules where appropriate to avoid breaking the continuity of a document with too much detail. The operative part of the document then refers to the schedule, and the schedule contains the detail. For example:

TENANT'S COVENANTS

The Tenant covenants with the Landlord to observe and perform the covenants set out in Schedule 1.

SCHEDULE 1

1. To pay the rent … etc.

Note that the obligation or right is created in the operative part of the document. Only the detail of the obligation or right is put in the schedule.

EXECUTION AND ATTESTATION

A document will end with an execution clause. This will refer to the signatures of the parties and any other formalities necessary to give the document legal effect. The wording of this clause will vary depending on the nature of the party executing, whether the document is executed as a deed, and whether the party's signature is witnessed ('attested').

For a document executed by an individual and not intended to take effect as a deed, the clause could read:

Signed by ALAN JONES)   **(Alan Jones**

in the presence of:)   **signs here)**

(Witness signs here)

If the document is intended to take effect as a deed the clause could read:

Executed as a deed)   **(Alan Jones**

by ALAN JONES)   **signs here)**

in the presence of:)

(Witness signs here)

Order of clauses in the operative part

It is difficult to lay down rules as to the order of clauses. It will vary according to the nature of the document, but is often a matter of common sense and logic.

CHRONOLOGICAL ORDER

One possibility is to list topics in chronological order. This is often particularly suitable for a document that deals with one simple transaction.

Imagine a contract for the hire of a car. The order of topics could be:

- parties;

- definitions;

- agreement by Owner to hire out car to Hirer on the terms set out in the agreement;

- payment;

- insurance;

- promises by Owner as to the state of the car at the start of the hire;

- duration of hire;

- what the car can be used for;

- who may drive;

- Hirer's promises as to the return of the car;

- remedies for breach of the agreement.

For a contract such as this, a chronological structure will produce a simpler and less repetitious document than if you try to divide topics into Owner's Obligations and Hirer's Obligations.

CATEGORICAL ORDER

A categorical structure sets out the duties and responsibilities in categories. An example of this is a lease.

The structure of a typical lease is:

- parties;

- definitions;

- the grant of the term by Landlord to Tenant;

- Tenant's covenants;

- Landlord's covenants;

- provisos, for example the Landlord's power to forfeit the lease.

Here, the division into landlord's obligations and tenant's obligations is essential. The obligations have to be performed throughout the entire term of the lease. There is no chronological order to them.

ORDER OF IMPORTANCE

This could be the order used in a simple contract, where the obligations are not to be carried out in any chronological order. An example could be an agreement between employer and employee on severance of employment.

A document may use a combination of these orders. A contract with a firm of furniture removers could list the firm's obligations in chronological order, for example:

- to pack the contents of the house;

- to transport to storage;

- to store;

- to transport to new house;

- to unpack;

and then list the owner's obligations.

In a lease, all the tenant's covenants will be put together, but will appear in order of importance.

1.2.4 Checking the draft

When you have finished the draft, check it carefully. To do this you must check:

- that it is carrying out your client's instructions, and that it is carrying out **all** of them. If you began by listing all the points that the document would have to cover, take the list and check off each item against the relevant clause;

- that the meaning of each sentence is unambiguous;

- the numbering of clauses;

- all cross-references in the document to other clauses or to schedules. References can easily become inaccurate if clauses are added to or deleted from the original draft;

- the headings to your clauses. Does the heading correctly represent the contents of the clause?

- the names of the parties;

- all figures and dates;

- spelling and grammar. Do not rely entirely on the 'spell check' on your computer. It will not reveal a mistake such as using 'principle' for 'principal'.

If possible, leave some time before making your final check. A fresh eye might spot mistakes previously overlooked.

1.2.5 Further points on drafting

Now that we have considered general principles, we shall look at particular points in more detail.

Definitions

USE OF DEFINITIONS

A definition can do two things.

It can create a '**tag**' or '**nickname**'. This avoids repetition of names or lengthy phrases. This use is seen in the description of the parties to a document. For example:

This agreement is made between

(1) Kingdom Finance plc [the Company]

(2) Edward Burns [the Borrower]

In the rest of the document it is only necessary to refer to the Company and the Borrower.

Another example is:

> **In this agreement**
>
> **1. 'the Period of Hire' means from 9am on 1 November 2002 until noon on 23 November 2002.**

Later clauses can then say things such as:

> **if the Hirer does not return the Car at or before the end of the Period of Hire ...**

It can create a private dictionary for the document by giving a word something other than its ordinary meaning, or by giving a word an unusually extended or restricted meaning.

For example:

> **In this agreement**
>
> **'Boat' includes a sailboard**

Note that it is usual to give the definition a capital letter, and use it with the capital letter throughout the document. This alerts anybody reading it to the fact that a particular word or expression has been given a particular meaning by the document.

WHERE TO PUT THE DEFINITIONS

Definitions that are to apply throughout the document should be put in alphabetical order in a definitions clause at the start of the operative part of the document.

> **DEFINITIONS**
>
> **In this Agreement**
>
> **(1) 'Arbitration' means ...**
>
> **(2) 'Balance Sheet' means ... etc**

If a definition will be used only in one part of a document or in one clause, you can put the definition at the start of the relevant part or clause.

> **4.1 In this clause, 'Promotional Material' means ...**
>
> **4.2 The Landowner must ensure that all Promotional Material is ...**

In a simple document, a 'tag' may be given to a name or phrase the first time that it is used, and the tag may then be used throughout the rest of the document. For example, in a contract for the sale of land, a clause may say:

> **The Seller, for the benefit of his adjoining property, 10 Smith Avenue, Morton, N. Yorks ('the Retained Land') reserves a right of way on foot ...**

Later clauses can then refer to the Retained Land.

This method should be used only for simple short documents. In a long document, it will be a waste of time to have to search through the clauses to find the one in which the tag was first bestowed.

SOME GROUND RULES FOR USING DEFINITIONS

1. Do not define a term if you are going to use the term in its ordinary dictionary meaning.

   For example, suppose that a person hiring a room is to be given a right to bring tables into it. If the owner of the room does not care what sort of the tables they are, do not define the word 'table'.

   However, if for some reason, only tables of a certain size are to be allowed, you could deal with this by a definition.

   In this agreement, 'Table' means a table that is no longer than two metres, and no wider than one metre.

   In such a simple example as this, it might be better not to use a definition but to restrict the right. In other words, instead of defining table, and later saying 'the Hirer may bring six Tables into the room', you could say:

   The Hirer may bring six tables into the room but no table may be longer than two metres or wider than one metre.

   It depends on whether or not you need a definition for other clauses.

2. A definition should only define. It should not be used to create a substantive right or obligation. The right or obligation should be created in the clause that uses the definition.

3. If you have a definition, do not forget to use it when you are drafting the rest of the document.

4. Whenever you use a defined term in a clause, check back to the definition. Does the definition make sense in this clause?

5. In a definition, do not define by reference to other undefined terms. For example,

   In this Agreement

   'Property' includes preliminary and reserved options.

   This definition may be meaningless without a definition of preliminary and reserved options.

Structuring a clause

STRUCTURING CLAUSES AND SUBCLAUSES WITHIN THE OPERATIVE PART

1. Use a separate clause for each separate matter.

2. Use sub-paragraphing to avoid long, cumbersome clauses and provisos.

   Consider:

   1. The Licensee shall purchase exclusively from the Grantor all materials used in making the Invention PROVIDED that the Licensee shall be entitled to relieve itself of its liability to observe this obligation upon giving the Grantor three months' notice in writing.

   Compare:

   1. Subject to Clause 2, the Licensee must purchase exclusively from the Grantor all materials used in making the Invention.

   2. The Licensee may end the obligation contained in Clause 1 by giving the Grantor three months' notice in writing.

3.   Number each clause and sub-clause.

4.   Give each clause or group of clauses a heading that correctly defines the subject matter of the clauses, eg:

Tenant's Covenants

STRUCTURING A CLAUSE ACCORDING TO COODE

Consider:

> **The Company shall reimburse the Replacement Value provided that the value of the claim does not exceed £1,000 and the Policyholder notifies the loss within 7 days from (but excluding) the date of its occurrence PROVIDED ALWAYS THAT the above shall not apply to claims made under Clause 10 of this Policy.**

This clause starts with a statement of a legal obligation which at first sight appears absolute. The conditions and exceptions attaching to the obligation are not stated until afterwards, so that it is necessary to reconsider the obligation in the light of them. This kind of clause construction is very common in legal drafting but it is not the most logical way to structure a clause and it makes it more difficult to understand.

In 1843, George Coode wrote a treatise on 'Legislative Expression'; or, 'The Language of The Written Law'. His general principle is that a clause should be structured in the following order:

- circumstances/exceptions (ie circumstances where the right or obligation does or does not exist);

- conditions (ie conditions on which the right or obligation depends);

- obligation or right (ie who **must** do what or who **may** do what).

Words suitable for introducing an exception are 'except where …'

Words suitable for introducing circumstances are 'where …' 'if … then' or 'when …' or 'on …'.

Words suitable for introducing conditions are 'if …' or 'provided that …'.

These are two examples of Coode in legislation.

Section 2(1) of the Land Registration and Land Charges Act 1971:

> '**If** any question arises as to whether a person is entitled to an indemnity under any provision of the Land Registration Act 1925 [*circumstance*] […] **he** [*person*] **may apply** to the court to have that question determined [*the right*].'

Section 23(1) of the Matrimonial Causes Act 1973:

> '**On** granting a decree of divorce … [*circumstance*] **the court** [*person*] **may make** any one or more of the following orders … [*right*].'

This is an example of Coode in a document.

15 Compensation on termination of contract

Except where otherwise provided [*exception*], if before 1 December 2001 this contract is terminated by the Buyer, [*circumstance*] then provided the Seller is not in breach of any of his obligations under this contract [*condition*] the Buyer must pay the Seller the sum of £5000 [*obligation*].

The rule produces a logical, and to lawyers, a familiar structure, but it does not have invariably to be followed.

Imagine that an owner of land has employed consultants to design and build an amusement park. The consultants want to control the use of their name in any advertising material issued by the landowner. Their name is to be used only if certain conditions are met.

If the clause were drafted using Coode's rule, it would read:

> **Only where**
>
> **(a)**   **the Landowner has given the Consultants advance details of any advertising material it plans to use; and**
>
> **(b)**   **the Consultants have given their express written approval; and**
>
> **(c)**   **the Consultants have not ended this Agreement under sub-clause 11(1)**
>
> **may the Landowner use the Consultant's name in advertising material.**

The clause could make the point in a more natural and in a stronger manner if Coode were ignored and the clause were drafted to read:

> **The Landowner may only use the Consultants' name in advertising material where:**
>
> **(a)**   **the Landowner has given the Consultants advance details of any advertising materials it plans to use; and**
>
> **(b)**   **the Consultants have given their express written approval; and**
>
> **(c)**   **the Consultants have not ended this Agreement under sub-clause 11(1).**

Layout and presentation of the document

PARAGRAPHS

Using paragraphs makes prose more readable and helps to avoid cumbersome clauses and sub-clauses.

TABULATION

Tabulation may help to avoid ambiguity.

Consider the sentence:

> **Any trainee solicitor is entitled to paid leave to attend a conference, lecture, or seminar *provided by The Law Society*.**

How much of the sentence is the phrase in italics intended to qualify? Does it apply only to 'seminar', or to 'conference' and 'lecture' as well?

Compare:

> **Any trainee solicitor is entitled to paid leave to attend:**
>
> **(a) a conference; or**
>
> **(b) a lecture; or**
>
> **(c) a seminar,**
>
> **provided by The Law Society.**

Care should be taken, however, not to indent the final phrase 'provided by The Law Society' to the same margin as 'a seminar' or the ambiguity would remain.

NUMBERING

Where a series of points is being made, numbering may improve clarity and aid later cross-referencing.

Examples of numbering systems:

4.5.1   The system adopted in this Resource Book and known as the decimal system.

4(5)(a)(i)   A system based on the legislative approach and known as the alpha-numeric system.

4.5(a)(i)   A combination system using elements of both decimal and alpha-numeric systems.

1.2.6 Use of precedents

A precedent is a good servant and a bad master. Do not start drafting from a precedent until you have analysed your client's instructions and decided what you want to achieve. If you turn to a precedent immediately, you will find that it controls you instead of being a helpful tool.

Using a precedent has the following benefits:

- the precedent might suggest a suitable structure for your document;

- it might suggest provisions that you have not thought of and that will benefit your client;

- it might suggest suitable wording;

- the introductory notes and footnotes might alert you to legal problems that you had not thought of.

It has the following perils:

- the precedent might suggest an unsuitable structure. In particular, it might tempt you into a long and complex document, when a simple one is all that is needed;

- it might tempt you to include clauses that are irrelevant, or worse, are to the disadvantage of your client;

- it might suggest inappropriate or archaic wording;

- the notes on law will lead you astray if the law has changed since the date the precedent was published.

Guidelines on the use of precedents

- Always decide what you want your document to do before you consider the precedents.

- Accept the fact there may be no precedent that exactly covers your situation.

- Adapt the precedent to your transaction; not your transaction to the precedent.

- Use modern precedents. Even modern precedents may have to be altered if the law has recently changed.

- Be careful if you bring a clause from a precedent into your draft document. The clause may have to be altered to follow the definitions in your draft, or to match its style or language. Sometimes, the clause which you bring in makes no sense without a definition in its parent document. Remember to alter the clause, or to bring in the definition as well.

- Do not copy words from a precedent unless you are sure of their legal effect.

- Do not change words in a precedent unless you are sure that the change will not have an unexpected legal effect. This is particularly true of precedents for wills.

- Be wary of using as a precedent a document which was drafted by someone else for some other transaction. The fact that a document has been used in another transaction does not necessarily make it a good precedent. Also, the document might have been slanted in favour of the party by whose solicitor it was drafted.

1.2.7 Language

Note: the following advice is applicable not only to the drafting of documents, but applies also to the writing of letters, reports and memoranda.

The following are sensible rules:

- use simple and direct language;

- keep sentences and paragraphs short;

- think before you use the passive;

- avoid ambiguity;

- be careful how you use 'shall' and 'will'.

Simple and direct language

'PADDING'

Try to avoid the use of unnecessary phrases which lengthen the sentence while adding nothing to its meaning. For example:

- 'until such time as';

- 'in this instance';

- 'the fact that';

- 'of course'.

TOO MANY ADJECTIVES?

Consider whether the noun requires an adjective at all. In the following examples, the adjective adds nothing to the noun:

- 'true facts';

- 'terrible disaster';

- 'unfilled vacancy'.

Try to avoid a string of similar adjectives which do not make the meaning more precise. For example:

- 'grave and fatal error';

- 'careful and detailed consideration'.

COMPOUND PREPOSITIONS

Try to avoid using a phrase where a single preposition will do. For example:

- 'in accordance with' (by, under);

- 'by reason of' (by, through);

- 'with reference to' (about);

- 'in order to' (to).

NOUNS DERIVED FROM VERBS

Could you use the verb itself rather than a noun derived from it? (This often creates a more immediate effect.)

- 'make an admission' (admit);

- 'give consideration to' (consider);

- 'effect a termination' (terminate or end);

JARGON

Try to avoid jargon unless you are sure the recipient will be familiar with it. For example:

- 'mortgage-sourcing information';

- 'clothing-optional beaches'.

'LEGALESE'

If possible, avoid archaic words and phrases such as:

- 'herewith';

- 'herein';

- 'hereinbefore';

- 'hereby';

- 'crave leave';

- 'the said …'.

LEGAL TERMS

Legal terms should be translated for lay clients. For example:

- 'joint tenancy';

- 'decree nisi'.

Short sentences and paragraphs

USE SHORT SENTENCES

In long sentences the verb, subject and object may be separated by too many sub-clauses. This places a strain on the reader's memory and understanding. Consider, for example:

> **The evidence, including evidence from independent surveys as well as that gathered personally by the writers of this report and the results of investigations formally commissioned by this department, suggests that the public, while acknowledging an overall increase in the actual level of government spending on health, by which is meant on health care both at the doctor–patient level and in hospitals, still views the problems and defects in the National Health Service and in particular in National Health hospitals as the result of a general lack of funding.**

The sub-clauses break up the main thought of the paragraph so that it is difficult to follow. The paragraph would be better rewritten in separate sentences with the main thought first, even though this may increase its length. Brackets can be used for subsidiary points where appropriate. For example:

> **The evidence suggests that the public still views the problems and defects in the National Health Service and in particular in National Health hospitals as the result of a general lack of funding. This is so even though it acknowledges an overall increase in the actual level of government spending on health care both at the doctor–patient level and in hospitals. (Evidence on this issue includes evidence from independent surveys, that gathered personally by the writers of this report and the results of investigations formally commissioned by this department.)**

Verbs in the passive

ACTIVE AND PASSIVE VOICE

In a sentence where the verb is in the active voice, the subject of the sentence acts upon the object of the sentence. Where the verb is in the passive voice, the object of the sentence is acted upon by the subject. Compare:

> **The defendant struck the claimant** (active voice).

> **The claimant was struck by the defendant** (passive voice).

PROBLEMS WITH THE PASSIVE

Over-use of the passive voice lengthens a sentence and can make it sound weak. In the worst cases, it obscures meaning. For example:

> **It is hoped that resources will be relocated so that changes may be made in the methods by which the system is administered.**

Where the verb is in the passive you may accidentally omit the phrase which indicates who or what is doing the acting. For example:

> **The claimant was struck.**

In a legal context, the effect of this omission may be important. For example:

> **Notice will be served.** By whom?

SOME USES FOR THE PASSIVE

The passive can sound more objective and detached and therefore more appropriate in certain legal contexts. For example:

The allegations are denied

sounds better than:

Our client denies the allegations, which introduces a personal note.

It is correct to use the passive where the subject of the legal action is irrelevant. For example:

The common seal of X Co was affixed ... It does not matter who affixed it.

The passive can also be used in a legal context to cover the possibility of action by a number of different persons, some of whom are unknown. For example:

If the goods are damaged we will refund the cost. This could cover damage by the supplier, the carrier, or any third party.

Ambiguity

TAKE CARE WITH WORD ORDER

Words or phrases in the wrong place may create ambiguity.

Consider the sentence:

We undertake to repair or replace goods shown to be defective *within six months of the date of purchase.*

It is not clear whether the phrase in italics governs the repair/replacement or the notification of defect. It could be rewritten as:

Where, within six months of the date of purchase, goods are shown to be defective, we will repair or replace them (assuming this was the intended meaning).

DO YOU MEAN 'AND' OR 'OR'?

Consider:

The Seller may serve notice of termination, recover goods already delivered and retain all instalments already paid.

The use of 'and' in this sentence suggests that the list is conjunctive, ie that the seller may do all of the things in it. But can he choose to do only some of them?

Compare:

The Seller may serve notice of termination, recover goods already delivered or retain all instalments already paid.

The use of 'or' here suggests that the list is disjunctive, ie that the seller may do only one of the things in the list. But it could also mean that he may *both* serve notice *and* either recover goods or retain instalments.

To avoid such ambiguity, consider (depending on the meaning required) using phrases such as:

The Seller may do all or any of the following:

or

The Seller may exercise one only of the following rights:

THE 'UNDISTRIBUTED MIDDLE'

Take care with provisions 'before/after' a particular date or 'over/under' a particular weight or measure.

Consider the following examples:

Where the company delivers the goods before 1 January ... / Where the company delivers the goods after 1 January ...

What happens if it delivers them *on* 1 January?

Goods over 40lb must be sent by rail ... / Goods under 40lb may be sent by air

What about goods weighing *exactly* 40lb?

EXPRESSIONS OF TIME

Take care to avoid ambiguity.

Consider:

The Buyer must pay a deposit within 7 days of today's date.

Does the 7 days include or exclude today?

For legal and practical reasons, avoid expressing periods of time in the following ways:

- from [a date];
- by [a date];
- within [so many days of] or from [a date];
- until [a date].

It is safer to be clear by using one of the following:

- from but excluding/not including;
- from and including;
- on or after;
- on or before;
- within a period of 7 days commencing with;
- until but excluding/not including;
- until and including.

ARE YOU CREATING AN OBLIGATION OR A DISCRETION?

An obligation is created by the phrase:

The Customer shall pay a deposit on signing this Agreement.

A discretion is created by the phrase:

The Company may retain the deposit if the Customer does not collect the goods on or before 30 June.

Take care when using 'shall'. It is grammatically correct to use it in the third person to indicate an obligation ('the Tenant shall pay the Rent') but it can also be used in the first person to indicate simple future ('I shall go to London'). Alternatively, you could use 'must' to create an obligation.

AVOID WORDS OF SIMILAR SOUND OR APPEARANCE

Words of similar sound or appearance can be accidentally transposed by a typist and may also confuse a lay client. For example:

Avoid	*Use instead*
'mortgagee/mortgagor'	'lender/borrower'
'lessor/lessee'	'landlord/tenant'

AMBIGUOUS PRONOUNS

Consider:

Where the Supplier fails to deliver the Goods to the Customer in accordance with Clause 9 or the Goods delivered do not correspond with the sample he may terminate this Agreement.

Who may terminate the agreement?

Where it is not clear to which noun a pronoun refers, the noun should be repeated.

THE EJUSDEM GENERIS RULE

Consider:

In consequence of war, disturbance or any other cause.

Unless a contrary intention appears, 'any other cause' will be construed as meaning only causes in the same category as those previously listed.

To avoid ambiguity, add (as appropriate):

whether of the same kind as [the causes] previously listed or not or

or any other [cause] provided it is of the same kind as the [causes] previously listed.

BLANKS

Try to minimise the number of blanks for completion to reduce the risk that they are left uncompleted.

Shall/will

In the first person, 'shall' simply looks to the future. In the second and third person, 'will' looks to the future.

I shall interview the client tomorrow. I hope that you will sit in. Afterwards, we shall discuss the drafting.

In the first person, 'will' expresses determination. In the second or third person, 'shall' expresses determination or obligation.

I will make you do this.

The Buyer shall pay £500 on the 1 December.

This means that you create problems if your document says 'the Buyer will pay ...'. Is this what he intends to do or is it what he is obligated to do?

Many documents use expressions such as 'If the Company shall breach this term ...'. The clause is looking to the future but is using 'shall' incorrectly. It could be redrafted to say 'In the event of the company breaking ...'. It is simpler to say 'If the Company breaks ...'.

1.2.8 Practical and ethical considerations when drafting

Good practice when submitting a draft

Out of courtesy, you should always supply to the other side an additional copy of any draft sent for approval.

Use a layout which helps the other side to read and amend the draft; for example, use wide margins and double spacing.

Good practice when amending the other side's draft

Amend a draft by hand so that the amendments are clear. Do not have the draft retyped or the amendments will become difficult for the other side to identify.

Do not erase another firm's word processor identification markings. It will be important for them to identify the disk quickly.

If you receive a draft which is substantially acceptable but in a style of drafting which you do not favour, it is tactless to redraft it in a different style and will not improve relations with that firm. The most you can do is to correct any errors and hope that any draft you send them in the future may influence them to change their style!

Ethical considerations when negotiating a draft

Two rules of professional conduct are relevant.

(1) A solicitor must not act, whether in his professional capacity or otherwise, towards anyone in a way which is fraudulent, deceitful or otherwise contrary to his position as a solicitor, nor must he use his position as a solicitor to take unfair advantage either for himself or another person.

(2) A solicitor must act towards other solicitors with complete frankness and good faith consistent with the overriding duty to his client.

Breach of these rules renders the solicitor liable to disciplinary action.

Do not attempt to mislead the other side by concealing amendments you have made to their draft, for example by writing a covering letter which draws attention to some amendments and not to others. Any deliberate attempt to mislead could be criminally fraudulent as well as amounting to professional misconduct.

Do not attempt to take advantage of a mistake made by the other side. Point it out to them. They may otherwise be able to claim rectification of the document to incorporate an omitted provision or allege that the agreement is a nullity, so enabling them to resist specific performance.

1.3 WRITING LETTERS

1.3.1 Who is the addressee?

Consider the needs of the reader and try to adapt your style accordingly.

The lay client

Take care to avoid jargon and legalese when writing to a lay client. Explain all unfamiliar terms, but try not to make the tone patronising. How familiar is the client with the subject?

The business client

The business client will generally be familiar with solicitors' letters, so avoid verbosity and get to the point quickly.

Other professionals

Other professionals may need some legal terms translated.

Other solicitors

What kind of matter are you dealing with? Are you writing from a position of strength or weakness? Do you want to adopt a conciliatory or non-conciliatory stance? Consider which is more likely to persuade the addressee. Remember that the other solicitor may send a copy of your letter to his client.

1.3.2 'Ghosting'

You may be asked to write letters to be signed in a partner's own name. Read the file and consider the partner's style. Check how well the partner knows the addressee; for example, if you are writing to a client, is the partner on first-name terms with him?

1.3.3 Starting and ending the letter

Generally

Letters beginning 'Dear Sirs/Sir/Madam' all end 'Yours faithfully'.

A letter addressed to a person by surname, for example 'Dear Mr Smith', ends with 'Yours sincerely'.

A letter beginning 'Dear John' may end with 'Yours sincerely' or 'Yours' (either of which could be prefixed by a phrase such as 'Kind regards' or 'Best wishes').

Female addressees

Where possible, try to find out a woman's preference in advance, for example 'Miss', 'Mrs', or 'Ms'. As an alternative, some writers use 'Dear Jane Smith' if 'Dear Madam' would be too formal and 'Dear Jane' too informal.

1.3.4 Content

Consider overall structure

An initial heading identifying the matter is conventional. For example:

Jones to Smith
Sale of 25 Acacia Avenue, Bristol

A complex letter will be easier to understand (and reply to) if you give each paragraph a number and a heading.

Form and style

If you are writing in the firm's name (eg a formal letter to the other side), write in the first person plural ('we') and be consistent.

Acknowledge the addressee's last communication.

If it is your first letter to the addressee, explain your involvement.

State the purpose of the letter.

Carry out that purpose using:

*   logical sequence;
*   separate paragraphs;
*   short sentences;
*   active voice.

Write in a restrained tone. Avoid over-emphasis (eg unnecessary adverbs – 'totally unhappy', 'completely inaccurate'). Rarely use exclamation marks. Do not express surprise, amazement, outrage, etc.

Avoid jokes and witticisms.

1.3.5 Some practical points

Second thoughts and improvements

Try to be detached about your letter. How will it appear through another's eyes?

How would it sound if read out in open court in the future?

Try not to write a letter in a temper or in an emotional state. If you do, do not post it until you have had a chance to re-read it or a colleague has reviewed it.

Consider giving a deadline for a reply (eg if the matter is urgent or if the letter might be unwelcome).

If you have asked a client to do something, are your instructions clear?

Check the grammar and spelling.

Final checks

Check that the letter:

- carries the correct references (ie yours and those of the other side);

- is dated;

- is signed;

- is accompanied by the right enclosures;

- is put into the right envelope, and is properly addressed.

1.4 WRITING REPORTS AND MEMORANDA

1.4.1 Reports

Purpose

Reports usually cover a specific subject and serve a particular purpose. In the office you may have to write a report on some legal research or fact-finding you were asked to undertake.

Is your research complete?

Consider whether you have all the necessary information and identify any gaps.

Edit your material

Consider how much information should go into the report. Brevity increases the likelihood of the report being read, but too little information may not adequately support your conclusions.

Planning your report

Plan the text of your report carefully to produce a logical argument.

Consider what will be the most useful structure for the reader. For example, if you were asked to answer specific questions could you use these to head paragraphs of your report?

Consider including:

- a contents page or index;

- an introduction explaining why the report was commissioned;

- a brief summary of the report before the main text for quick reference;

- diagrams (if relevant);

- case or statute references (if relevant);

- a bibliography;

- appendices;

- acknowledgments of sources of information.

Style

For whom are you writing? Adapt your style appropriately.

Consider whether you should paraphrase or explain your source material, or whether you can reproduce it word for word.

Layout and presentation

Make sure the report is well set out, with clear headings and numbered paragraphs and sub-paragraphs if appropriate.

Is it to be used as a discussion document? If so, consider having it typed in double spacing with wide margins to leave room for others to write notes.

Final checks

Have the report typed in draft form first. Read it through carefully, amending and rewriting where necessary.

Check that you have:

• done what you were asked to do;

• identified any relevant options;

• reached a conclusion.

1.4.2 Memoranda

Types of memoranda

Solicitors generally have to write two types of memoranda:

• attendance notes (as a record of their meetings or telephone calls with clients, other solicitors, etc);

• internal memoranda (as a quick way of communicating with others in the firm).

Attendance notes

Attendance notes are put on a file as a record of an oral discussion, transaction or agreement and must be clear and accurate in case of any later dispute.

They are essential for anyone who takes over a file and was not present for the meeting, telephone call, etc.

They may also be needed when a client's bill is prepared as part of the record of chargeable time spent on the matter.

Write or dictate your attendance note as soon as possible after the event it records so as to avoid forgetting essential detail.

Always try to take contemporaneous notes – in a simple case you can put them straight on the file. For more complicated matters, you can use your notes to compile your attendance note, but do not destroy them; they are important additional evidence in any dispute.

An attendance note should normally contain the following:

- the client's name;
- the subject matter;
- your reference;
- the date;
- the place (of any meeting);
- the people present (at a meeting);
- the starting and finishing times (of the meeting or phone call);
- a summary of what was discussed or agreed;
- any follow-up action to be taken by you or others.

If your attendance note records an important decision or agreement, always confirm it by letter to avoid misunderstandings.

Internal memoranda

Keep internal memoranda brief and business-like, but take care with the tone. If a memo sounds curt, you may cause offence to the recipient.

The format required is generally as follows:

MEMORANDUM

From:

To:

Fee earner's reference:

Date:

Client's name:

Client's matter:

File number:

Most firms use printed forms on which these headings already appear.

1.5 EMAIL

Email is often a convenient substitute for telephone conversations, exchange of memoranda and informal letters. Also it is a quick and relatively cheap method of transmitting documents.

Email has many benefits. It is a good substitute for the telephone when the same message needs to be communicated to several people. It also overcomes the frustration of trying to speak to someone who is never available to answer the telephone.

However, there are drawbacks. As emails tend to be short and to the point, they can sound curt. Therefore, care is needed when they are addressed to clients and indeed other members of staff. It is always wise to print off and read the message before it is sent. Where the email relates to a client's matter, remember to keep a hard copy on the file.

There are further problems with ensuring confidentiality and also checking the authenticity of incoming emails. Your firm may have a policy on email usage and the Law Society has issued guidelines (which can be found on the Law Society website www.Lawsociety.org.uk).

1.6 FURTHER READING

Melville *Draftsman's Handbook* (Longman, 1991)
Robinson *Drafting* (Butterworths, 1980)
Berg *Drafting Commercial Agreements* (Butterworths, 1991)
Aitken *Piesse – The Elements of Drafting* 9th edn (LBC Information Services, 2001)
Gowers *The Complete Plain Words* (Penguin, 1987)
Fowler's *Modern English Usage* (Oxford University Press, 1983)
Adler *Clarity for Lawyers* (The Law Society, 1990)
Thomas *Plain English for Lawyers* (National Consumer Council, 1990)

PART II

PRACTICAL LEGAL RESEARCH

Chapter 2

INTRODUCTION TO PRACTICAL LEGAL RESEARCH

2.1 WHY SHOULD I READ THIS SECTION?

Many of you will be thinking that you can do legal research already. This may be true. Undoubtedly at some time or other you will have located and summarised a primary source. Some of you will have presented long and detailed essays on legislative history or on the differing opinions of learned members of the judiciary. Some of you may even have kept the mountain of photocopied guides to legal research handed out during the undergraduate degree or the GDL. Whilst the experiences you will have gathered so far are undoubtedly useful, on their own they do not equip you to do this course or, more importantly, to conduct research in practice. The following chapters are therefore designed to build on your existing skills by switching the focus from academic study to practical application.

2.2 LEGAL RESEARCH IN THE OFFICE

Law firms exist to make money. As a trainee you will almost certainly be required to generate fees. You will do this by selling your time. Of equal importance, you will almost certainly be required to support other fee earners in their quest to charge fees. The skill of practical legal research is of particular importance in this regard. To be blunt, a principal task of a trainee is to conduct legal research for other people! To be even more blunt, your ability to impress the people for whom you conduct research will be a key factor in whether you succeed or fail in your career as a solicitor.

In the context of practical legal research, this means producing work that is:

- accurate;
- carried out efficiently;
- commercially aware; and
- presented in an appropriate form.

2.3 LEGAL RESEARCH SKILLS: A MODEL

Legal research skills involve the ability to find and report the relevant material in the quickest possible time. There is no mechanical formula that will enable you to do this. Practice is the only way to achieve competence. However, the following general stages should be borne in mind.

2.3.1 Analyse the problem

Producing a brilliant piece of work that does not answer the question will win you nothing. The first stage of research is to analyse the problem carefully. Does it involve a single issue, or a number of related issues? Are they issues of substantive law, or issues of procedure? Work out exactly what it is that you are required to do. Work out what factual information you already have, and what information you will require. If in doubt, check with the person who set the task!

2.3.2 Consider what law might be relevant

As you will see from the following chapters, the vast majority of research tools (paper or electronic) require the use of keywords. When starting their research many students make the mistake of being too specific as to the information they search for. A particularly common mistake when conducting legal research is to attempt to find precedent which exactly matches the detailed facts of the problem.

> *Example*
> Imagine that your supervisor has a client who is complaining that she has ordered a colour television from a shop but the shop has delivered a black and white television. The supervisor asks you to investigate possible remedies. One way of tackling this problem is to do a keyword search using the word 'televisions'. This is not the best way of going about the search. A better approach would be to research the underlying law which might be relevant. Hence the more able student would probably start their search with areas such as:
>
> – contract remedies;
> – sale of goods;
> – unfair terms in consumer contracts.

2.3.3 Identify the correct sources

Having read the above example, some of you may be thinking that you have to have considerable knowledge about the relevant areas of law before beginning the research. This is not the case. The key to success lies in selecting the most appropriate resource to begin with.

As a general rule, it is usually a good idea to start with a source which gives a general overview of the relevant laws first. A popular publication in this regard is *Halsbury's Laws of England*. However, it is stressed that this is not the only publication available. You should consider key practitioners' texts and also your own textbooks as a good overview source of law.

Once you have a good idea as to which laws might be relevant, you should consider moving on to a second layer of research tools, those which contain the primary sources. Primary sources include statutes, statutory instruments and case-law. Many students are somewhat nervous about using primary sources. There is no need to be nervous. Although sometimes the language is difficult, primary sources are essential to your research as they contain an authoritative assessment of what the law actually is rather than what it should be.

It is worth remembering that there are hundreds of different sources of legal information. Some are in paper form; some are in electronic form; some are in both. Each source has different strengths and weaknesses. The following sections of this Resource Book will familiarise you with some of the main sources. Think carefully about which source to use for a particular problem. If you choose wrongly, the research will take far longer and your results may be inaccurate.

2.3.4 Record the research trail

When conducting legal research in practice three things will very often happen:

- the facts might change, requiring the conclusions drawn from the legal research to be reviewed again;
- your supervisor may want to check your work; and
- your client or the courts may want proof that the work you are charging for has actually been done.

For each of these reasons (and for a myriad of others) it is vital to record the information found and the methods used to locate it very carefully and using the correct citations.

2.3.5 Update your information

The law changes constantly. You should therefore make sure that the law you find is as up to date as possible. This is explained further in the following chapters.

2.3.6 Presenting your findings in an appropriate format

You should also present your findings in writing where possible. It is, however, important to remember that your supervisor is undoubtedly a busy person. You will soon learn how your supervisor likes their reports to be presented but in most cases they will not thank you for producing armfuls of law reports and statutes without a least attempting to draw some conclusions from your research. Whatever structure you adopt it is always a good idea to put a summary of your findings at the top of the report.

2.3.7 Know when to stop and ask

With so much law out there, it is sometimes very difficult to spot that you have found the correct answer when it is right in front of you. Remember what was said right at the beginning of this chapter about accuracy and efficiency. Getting the correct answer is very important; however, so is making the most efficient use of your time. If you think that you have found the correct answer or if you are getting stuck then stop the research and go back to your supervisor with what you have done so far. Ask the supervisor for guidance, it is what he or she is there for!

2.3.8 Summary – tips for success

- analyse the problem(s) carefully so that you are certain as to your objectives;
- consider relevant law;
- select the most appropriate research tool and learn to use the tools properly – do not cut corners!
- always update your information;
- present the information in an appropriate form;
- do not be afraid to ask for help.

2.4 USING INDEXES

An effective way to access the information content in a source is to use an index. Most sources (paper and electronic) will have one or more 'tables of primary sources', and a 'subject index'. A table of primary sources is an index that helps you to locate cases, statutes or statutory instruments appearing in a work. It is also useful for completing or correcting a flawed citation. Arrangement may be alphabetical or chronological. A subject index helps you to locate commentary on specific areas of the law. Often this commentary will refer to primary sources, either in the text itself or in footnotes.

Using a subject index in a paper source is an acquired skill. Look at any index to see how it is arranged. There may be entries in this form:

county court

  jurisdiction

    extent

The broad topic, **county court**, appears first. Subsequent entries are progressively more specific. To make best use of the index, you need to look up the appropriate keyword that will lead to the specific answer to your problem. Looking under **extent** would probably be too narrow to include a reference to county courts. A good index will offer a variety of terms, including references between synonyms. However, choosing the right term will always involve a process of elimination, and some inspired guesswork.

Electronic databases often allow you to search for terms appearing anywhere in a source. In other words, their 'subject index' comprises every word appearing in the source. This facility, known as a 'free text' search, is quick and powerful. However, it can generate large numbers of irrelevant results (for example, instances where your search term happens to appear in discussion of a different subject). Often it is more effective to search within a particular field of the entries in an electronic source, such as 'case party' or 'catchwords' in a database of law reports. Searching an electronic database also requires you to be alert to possible synonyms. For example, if you search for 'employment law' but the preferred term used in the source is 'labour law', the database may generate zero results although there is actually plenty of coverage of the subject.

2.5 UPDATING

2.5.1 Why update?

Developments may occur at any time in any area of the law. The practitioner has a duty to keep up to date in order to give effective advice to the client. Updating your research must therefore become a matter of routine. Update even when a source seems to provide a satisfactory answer.

2.5.2 What developments are likely?

Consider what kinds of developments are most likely to have occurred in relation to your research. For example, is this an area that generates a large volume of case-law, affecting earlier cases or affecting the interpretation of a statute? Is it an area where the law can be changed by statutory instrument? Is it likely that relevant new legislation has been recently enacted? A thorough update will check for all these possibilities, but the efficient researcher will check the most likely developments first.

2.5.3 General procedure

Subsequent chapters will give details of how to update using particular sources. The procedure does vary. However, the following general points should be borne in mind:

- note the information that is to be updated, with full references;
- note the publication date of the source of the information (electronic databases may be continually updated, so there is no static 'publication date'; in this case, make clear the date that you carried out your search);
- check for an indication of the date to which the source claims that the law stated is current (again this may not be explicit in relation to an electronic database);
- stay with the original source until it ceases to be useful; for example, if the information has been found in a textbook, check whether any supplement exists;
- become familiar with tools whose main purpose is updating (for example, case citators and legislation citators);
- when switching sources, always compare the scope of content; if unfamiliar with a new source, look for an explanatory preface, user guide or online help facility;
- continue to make notes of new information and references as the investigation progresses.

Current Law is the most general updating source available. The paper version comprises several components. These will be described in the context of different research tasks in subsequent chapters. The content of *Current Law* is also available as part of the *Westlaw* subscription database.

2.6 FURTHER READING

Clinch *Using a Law Library: a Student's Guide to Legal Research Skills* 2nd edn (Blackstone, 2001)

Dane and Thomas *How to Use a Law Library: an Introduction to Legal Skills* 4th edn (Sweet & Maxwell, 2001)

Holborn *Butterworths Legal Research Guide* 2nd edn (Butterworths, 2001)

Chapter 3

ELECTRONIC VERSUS PRINTED SOURCES

3.1 INTRODUCTION

Law libraries no longer comprise printed materials alone. Paper sources are increasingly supplemented by 'virtual' libraries of electronic documents. In some cases, digital alternatives have overtaken printed sources altogether. This leads to improved currency of information, more flexible searching, and often the facility to access information from a computer at home. Depending on the content of your research, you may find that electronic sources become your tool of first resort, and that you refer to paper sources as a supplement, rather than the other way around.

On the other hand, printed materials continue to play a key role in legal research. Many significant sources continue to be available in paper form only. Cost may be a limiting factor in provision of electronic sources in practice (subscriptions to databases are expensive, and significant investment in hardware is also required). In many instances, it is simply more convenient to consult a paper source.

You need to know how to exploit a range of sources in paper and electronic format in order to become a competent legal researcher. Where there is a choice of formats, select according to which is most suited to the task in hand.

3.2 CD-ROM VERSUS INTERNET

A CD-ROM is a compact disc that holds a large volume of digital information. It is portable, and can be used on any personal computer that has a CD drive. In practice, CD-ROMs will often be loaded on a central computer so that their content can be accessed by any machine connected to the office network.

An online database is a collection of digital information that is accessed remotely (ie it is held on a computer outside the office, and often outside the country where the office is located). The gateway to the source is the internet. Some legal online databases can be accessed for free. Others entail payment of a subscription, and require a password. Sometimes this subscription is a one-off annual fee. Premium resources may charge according the length of each research session (in which case the pressure is on to search efficiently to be cost-effective!).

Often sources are available to buy in CD-ROM and online format. However, the two versions are not necessarily identical, if only because online databases are usually updated more often. For reasons of currency and flexibility, online is becoming the preferred format for providing electronic information.

3.3 ADVANTAGES OF ELECTRONIC SOURCES

- Often accessible from outside the office;
- simultaneous access by many users to single source;
- high volumes of information can be stored efficiently;
- speed of updating by publisher;
- quick, flexible and efficient searching and retrieval;
- ability to manipulate text (for example, cut and paste key passages from source).

3.4 ADVANTAGES OF PRINTED SOURCES

- Straightforward to access (no need for passwords, or training in search software);
- easy on the eye (people do not like to read more than a couple of pages of information on screen);
- costs associated with electronic information are generally high;
- not affected by technological failure;
- convenience (for example, quick reference/to read on the train home);
- easy to compare two or more sources at the same time;
- easy to scan/browse by 'flicking through'.

3.5 BASIC RULES FOR SEARCHING ELECTRONIC DATABASES

3.5.1 The basic commands

There are certain basic commands whose function is universal when searching electronic databases. Some allow you to combine separate search terms in different ways. Others allow you to search for varieties of the same term in one go. The most important commands are:

- **AND** – combining two terms with 'and' causes the computer to retrieve only those documents where both the first term and the second term appear; narrows down a search

  eg donoghue **and** stevenson

- **OR** – combining two terms with 'or' causes the computer to retrieve all documents where the first term appears, and also all documents where the second term appears; expands a search; useful for synonyms

  eg fence **or** boundary

- **NOT** – combining two terms with 'not' causes the computer to retrieve documents that contain the first term, but do not contain the second term; narrows down a search

  eg pollution **not** air

- * (asterisk) – commonly used at the end of a term as a truncation symbol; causes the computer to retrieve documents that contain varieties of the term based on a common word-stem; expands a search eg neglig* (will retrieve occurrences of negligent/negligently/negligence/negligée)

- ! (exclamation mark) – wildcard symbol used in the middle of a term; causes the computer to retrieve documents that contain terms with different internal spelling; expands a search

  eg wom!n (will retrieve occurrences of women and woman)

The commands AND, OR and NOT are sometimes known as Boolean operators or connectors.

3.5.2 Potential traps

Unfortunately, publishers of electronic databases use different versions of software. It is especially important to understand how these differences affect searching. Some traps for the unwary include:

- treatment of phrases: sometimes you need to enter the phrase alone; sometimes you need to enclose the phrase in inverted commas to achieve the same result;
- case sensitivity: some databases will search for terms in the same way whether or not you use capitals, others will respond differently; in some instances, case sensitivity applies to Boolean connectors (for example, these connectors must be entered in upper case in Butterworths Direct databases to be recognised as such);
- abbreviations: some databases demand full stops in abbreviations (for instance, B.B.C.), others ignore this; for this reason, avoid searching for cases in the form of 'smith v jones' – instead search for both parties as separate terms, combined with the connector AND.

3.5.3 Information overload

Information overload is a common problem when researching with electronic sources. Searching a database of case-law with a single broad term such as 'nuisance' will generate hundreds of hits; searching a general internet search engine such as *Google* or *AltaVista* may retrieve millions of different websites. The source you need will probably be in the middle of these results, and you will never find it.

Learn to use the commands described above to save time, by giving precision and structure to your searching. Learn about the quirks of the software used by different databases (most feature an on-screen help facility, and many offer on-screen tutorials). Finally, be cautious about using 'free text' search facilities. A free text search asks the computer to retrieve documents that contain your search term(s) anywhere within their text. This is the scattergun approach – it is comprehensive, but it is likely to generate a large proportion of results that are irrelevant to your purpose. Usually it is more effective to opt to search within a particular field of documents (eg case party names, subject keywords, etc).

Chapter 4

GETTING STARTED

4.1 INTRODUCTION

Assume that you have completed your preliminary analysis of the relevant facts and identified the legal issues involved in your problem. You now need to research the law in detail and consider how it applies to the circumstances before you.

It is unwise to refer to primary sources straightaway, even if you think you understand the appropriate branch of law thoroughly. Begin with a source that offers a general statement of the law in your area of interest, in order to map out an overview of the issues involved. Ideally the coverage of this source will be comprehensive, its style will be concise, and it will give detailed references to primary sources, perhaps in footnotes.

Such commentary will be found in legal encyclopedias and practitioner books. *Halsbury's Laws of England*, an extensive general encyclopedia, is usually a good starting point. It surveys the whole of the law of England and Wales, including relevant European provisions. Alternatively, books aimed at practitioners offer detailed coverage of a variety of specialised subjects.

4.2 *HALSBURY'S LAWS OF ENGLAND*

The printed version of *Halsbury's Laws of England* runs to 56 volumes, plus updating material. Alternatively, the full text is available online as *Halsbury's Laws Direct*.

Halsbury's Laws of England covers the present state of all areas of English law. It is arranged alphabetically by subject. Each subject is divided into numbered paragraphs that summarise the law in a particular area. Footnotes direct you to related cases and statutes.

4.2.1 Using the paper version

To find out the law using the paper version of *Halsbury's Laws of England*, you must take four steps:

- index,
- main volumes,
- cumulative supplement, and
- noter-up.

HOW TO USE *HALSBURY'S LAWS OF ENGLAND*

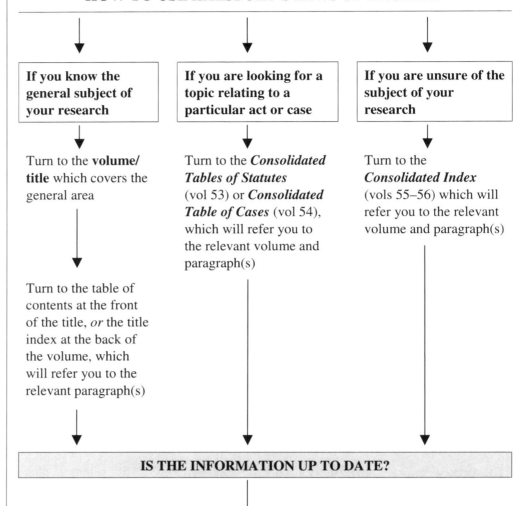

If you know the general subject of your research

Turn to the **volume/ title** which covers the general area

Turn to the table of contents at the front of the title, *or* the title index at the back of the volume, which will refer you to the relevant paragraph(s)

If you are looking for a topic relating to a particular act or case

Turn to the *Consolidated Tables of Statutes* (vol 53) or *Consolidated Table of Cases* (vol 54), which will refer you to the relevant volume and paragraph(s)

If you are unsure of the subject of your research

Turn to the *Consolidated Index* (vols 55–56) which will refer you to the relevant volume and paragraph(s)

IS THE INFORMATION UP TO DATE?

Look in the annual hardback *Cumulative Supplement* for your volume and paragraph number. An entry means the law has changed between the publication date of the volume and the operative date of the *Cumulative Supplement.*

Then look in the *Noter-up* section of the **Current Service Noter-up** binder for your volume and paragraph numbers. An entry means the law has changed since the operative date of the *Cumulative Supplement.*

(a) Index

The 'consolidated index' (vols 55–56) identifies and gives references to keywords. Think of subject terms that identify the problem you are researching. The index will refer you from those terms to discussion of the law in one or more of the main volumes:

> eg CROSSBOW
> *meaning*, **11(1)**, 170n
> birds, prohibition for protection of, **2**, 338 …

Each reference indicates the context in which crossbows are being discussed, followed by the number in **bold** of the main volume where the discussion appears, and then the paragraph (*not* the page) number. If the paragraph number is followed by 'n', the reference is to a footnote to that paragraph. Footnotes often refer to relevant cases and statutory provisions.

Make an accurate note of the reference, so that you can find it again easily in future, then locate the relevant main volume and paragraph.

(b) Main volumes

The 52 'main volumes' give a statement of the law of England and Wales, arranged by subject. Volume 1 begins with administrative law. Volume 50 ends with the law of wills. Volumes 51–52 are concerned with aspects of European Community law that are relevant to English law. Each volume has its own subject index at the back.

(c) Cumulative supplement

Over the years, the main volumes are reissued on a rolling programme. Therefore you must always check that the information in your main volume is up to date.

This updating process involves two stages. To begin with, consult the annual two-volume 'cumulative supplement'. The content of this is up to date to 31 October preceding its year of publication (the year of publication is printed on the spine). Any developments affecting your area of law since publication of the main volumes are likely to feature here. Entries appear under the same volume and paragraph references as in the main volumes.

(d) Noter-up

Finally, check the 'noter-up' in binder 2 of the looseleaf 'current service'. Updated monthly, this will alert you to any very recent changes in the law. Once again, look under the volume and paragraph number of your original reference. If any developments are listed, short summaries will be found in the appropriate 'monthly review' in binder 1.

4.2.2 Using the electronic version

Scope

Halsbury's Laws Direct features the electronic full text of vols 1–50 of *Halsbury's Laws of England* (ie excluding the two main volumes that deal with European law). It also includes the updating material contained in the latest annual cumulative supplement and monthly noter-up. It is a Butterworths subscription database.

Navigation

The front screen features direct links to separate parts of the database on the right (permitting access by browsing) and various search facilities on the left.

The usual screen layout is split. A contents list appears on the left, allowing you to jump to another point in the encyclopedia at any time. The full text appears on the right. This comprises a main window, and a separate narrower section beneath headed 'update' in blue. The main window reproduces the content of the corresponding main volume of the paper publication. The update section features any relevant updating content from the latest annual cumulative supplement and monthly noter-up. **It is essential to read both to establish the current state of the law.**

Searching

To *browse* coverage of a particular subject, click *browse Halsbury's Laws of England*. A contents list appears on the left of the screen. Click the '+' symbols at various levels of the contents list. When you reach an appropriate section, click its heading to produce the full text on the right of the screen.

To *search* across the text of the encyclopedia, you have various options. The recommended option is *Subject Search*. Click the button with this name. Enter the keyword(s) you wish to search for in the box at the top of the screen. If you enter more than one word, specify in the 'search how' box below whether these should appear 'next to each other in order' (ie as a phrase) or 'in any order in the same paragraph'.

4.3 PRACTITIONER BOOKS

In the office you would not normally refer to student textbooks or other academic works. These are not primarily intended to assist a thorough and pragmatic assessment of the law relating to a particular issue in hand. Practitioner books are intended to fulfil this role.

Practitioner books are written for, and usually by, practising lawyers. They give detailed and comprehensive coverage of an area of the law, with special emphasis on practice and procedure. As such, currency is an important concern. Publishers use different methods to keep practitioner books up to date. It is important that you understand which method is appropriate to sources you may use:

- a new edition may be published annually (for example in relation to revenue law, where the Budget brings about extensive changes each year);
- paperback supplements may appear during the lifetime of an edition; these accumulate updates to particular pages or paragraphs in the main work that have been superseded by changes in the law;
- the looseleaf format permits single pages or sections to be replaced regularly, thus integrating developments into the main work itself.

Most practitioner works (or their supplements) will print a date to which the law that they state is current. This date is usually found in the preface, or some other introductory section. Where they exist, electronic versions of practitioner works will be updated as frequently as the editors can manage; for an internet source, this may be daily, but for a CD-ROM source, it may only be monthly or even quarterly. You may have to look hard for a clear commitment as to how up to date the content of an electronic database is claimed to be!

Mention should also be made of precedent books. These assist practitioners in the drafting of documents, by giving examples of structure and wording that can be adapted for use in a given matter. Annotations often explain the effect of particular wording, and may cite relevant authorities. The two major collections of precedents are *Atkin's Encyclopedia of Court Forms in Civil Proceedings* (available in paper form only) and *The Encyclopedia of Forms and Precedents* (covering non-litigious matters; available in paper form and electronic form).

Chapter 5

RESEARCHING CASE-LAW

5.1 HOW ARE CASES PUBLISHED?

Judgments delivered in court are published via a number of channels. The most rapid of these is the internet. For example, the raw texts of selected judgments of the Court of Appeal are published on the free website of the Court Service on the day that they are handed down (see http://www.courtservice.gov.uk). Another useful free site that gathers judgments from a variety of UK courts is *BAILII* (the British and Irish Legal Information Institute – see http://www.bailii.org). A large archive of transcripts of judgments can also be accessed via the subscription database *Lawtel*.

Commercial publishers then add value to their reports of judgments in various ways, such as provision of summaries ('headnotes') and tables of cases referred to. These series of reports should be your preferred source of case-law. They are usually available in paper form, often available in electronic form, and sometimes available in both.

Reports are published regularly in *The Times* and *The Independent* newspapers. Case notes also appear in weekly practitioners' journals, such as *New Law Journal* and *Solicitors' Journal*. Some series of reports are intended to cover cases in specialist areas (for example, *Road Traffic Reports* and *Family Law Reports*). Finally, three general series feature the most significant cases across the law: *All England Reports*, *Weekly Law Reports* and (confusingly named) the *Law Reports*.

5.2 THE *LAW REPORTS* AND THE *WEEKLY LAW REPORTS*

The *Law Reports* are published by the Incorporated Council of Law Reporting for England and Wales. They are the nearest to an official series of case reports for this jurisdiction. Reports are checked by the presiding judge before publication. **Always cite the *Law Reports* in preference to any other series if possible.**

The *Law Reports* have been published continuously in various parallel series since 1865. The names of these series have changed frequently over the years, in line with the shifting structure of divisions of the courts. There are currently four separate series: Appeal Cases (abbreviated to AC); Chancery Division (Ch); Family Division (Fam); and Queen's Bench Division (QB).

The *Weekly Law Reports* are also published by the Incorporated Council, appearing in three volumes annually. Judgments in volumes 2 and 3 are intended for revision and later republication in the *Law Reports*, so that the two series complement one another. Volume 1 contains less important cases, including cases likely to go to appeal.

5.3 CITATION OF CASES

In order to locate the report of a case, you often need to interpret its citation. Citations identify cases by notation, referring to a volume and page in a particular series of law reports. A typical citation for an English case is:

[1963] 2 QB 744

This tells you that the report of the case of *Jordan v Burgoyne* starts at p 744 of vol 2 of the Queen's Bench series of the *Law Reports* for 1963.

Certain conventions underpin the system of citation. Note that the year in this instance appears in square brackets. That is because it is essential for locating the case. Volumes of the *Law Reports* are consecutively numbered within each year only, not from year to year. By contrast the case of *Bowker v Rose* is reported in (1977) 121 SJ 274. Volumes of *Solicitors' Journal* are consecutively numbered from year to year. Therefore you can find this case simply by knowing that it is in vol 121. The year is strictly superfluous, and so it appears in round brackets.

Another convention is the use of abbreviations to stand for titles of series of law reports, such as 'QB' and 'SJ'. These can be confusing. Most modern abbreviations are listed in *Current Law* (see the front of any *Monthly Digest* or *Year Book*) and at the front of vol 1 of *The Digest*. For a comprehensive list, see Raistrick *Index to Legal Citations and Abbreviations* 2nd edn (Bowker, 1993).

5.3.1 Neutral citation

At the beginning of 2001, a new system of common citation was introduced for cases in the High Court, the Court of Appeal and the House of Lords. This system is 'neutral' as regards format and publisher. In other words, it identifies cases by a unique reference, independent of the series of reports in which they are reproduced, and independent of whether they appear online or in print. The new arrangements supplement rather than replace the conventions described above. For further details, see *Practice Note (Judgments: Neutral Citation)* [2001] 1 All ER 193.

5.4 INCOMPLETE CITATIONS

If you have a citation, this should be enough to locate the report of a case, even if you do not know the names of the parties concerned. However, how do you locate a report if all that you know is the names of the parties?

Where the subject matter of the case is known, try checking the table of cases in a relevant practitioner book or student textbook. If this is unsuccessful, use the *Current Law Case Citator* if the case was decided since 1947 (or if you are unsure when the case was decided). Otherwise use *The Digest*.

5.4.1 *Current Law Case Citator*

The *Current Law Case Citator* is an index of cases by party. Coverage is comprehensive, beginning in 1947. It is available in paper form, and as part of the *Westlaw* subscription database.

The printed set comprises several volumes covering different date ranges (1947–1976; 1977–1997; annual supplements for recent years). Start with the earliest volume and work forwards. For very recent cases, consult the 'cumulative table of cases' near the back of the latest issue of the *Monthly Digest* (no need to look in earlier issues for the same year!).

One of the functions of the citator is to give full references to enable you to locate reports of the case. It will also refer you to a summary of the case in the relevant *Current Law Year Book*. For example:

> *Foster v Tyne and Wear CC* [1986] 1 All ER 567, CA ... Digested, 86/**1067**

This case is 'digested' or summarised in the *Current Law Year Book* of 1986, at para 1067.

To search for references to reports of a case using *Westlaw*, go to the home page and enter one or more names in the 'Search by Party Name(s)' box. Click 'go'. A list of search results, with citations, will appear in grey on the left of the screen.

5.4.2 *The Digest*

The Digest is a multi-volume encyclopedia. It indexes and summarises over 500,000 cases, in an alphabetical subject arrangement. Irish, Scottish, Commonwealth and European Community cases are covered, as well as English cases. It is especially useful for tracing older cases (although its coverage extends to the present). Look up the first party in the *Consolidated Table of Cases* volumes at the end of the set. An entry here will refer you to a main volume. Look up the party again in the 'table of cases' at the front of that volume. This will refer you to a paragraph within the volume. The paragraph will summarise the case and give a list of citations to full reports.

5.5 UPDATING CASES

Once you have found your case you must always check if it is still good law. *The Digest* does this job of reporting developments by the 'annotations' section of each case summary. However, the best source for the subsequent judicial history of a case is the *Current Law Case Citator*. (If the case pre-dates 1947 it is still worth checking the citator, since consideration in a post-1947 judgment qualifies an older case for inclusion.)

The procedure is to find the earliest reference to the case, then check the case lists in later volumes (and the latest issue of the *Monthly Digest*) for subsequent developments. Here is an example of an entry in the paper version of the citator:

> *R v Blackburn (James)* (1979) 1 Cr App R (S) 205, CA Digested, 81/**525**: Considered, 87/1035: Cited, 89/1071: Referred to, 84/880: Distinguished, 88/977

The case of *R v Blackburn* is summarised, or 'digested', in the *Current Law Year Book* of 1981, at para 525. It has been treated in various ways in subsequent decisions that are also summarised. The references 'considered, 87/1035', etc are to paragraphs in later year books.

If you are searching for developments using *Westlaw*, you can check across all years covered in one go. At the home page, enter one or more names in the 'Search by Party Name(s)' box. Click 'go'. A list of search results appears in grey on the left of the screen. To view a summary of a listed case, including any references in subsequent judgments, click the blue number next to the party names. Any developments are listed below the summary, in a section headed 'citations to the case'.

5.6 FINDING CASES ON A SUBJECT

Cases on a particular topic may be traced using a general source, such as *Halsbury's Laws of England* or a relevant practitioner book (see Chapter 4: *Getting Started*). Another useful printed source is *The Digest*.

Electronic databases are very effective for subject searching, since they offer the facility to search for occurrences of keywords anywhere in the text they contain. However, beware of information overload! Until you are skilled in carrying out such 'free text' searches, you may find that you generate large numbers of results, many of which are irrelevant to your purpose.

5.6.1 Using *The Digest* to find cases on a subject

The Digest is arranged alphabetically by subject. It is therefore well suited to identifying cases that deal with a particular topic.

The procedure is to look up your topic in the paperback 'consolidated index'. An entry here will refer you to the volume, subject heading and paragraph numbers where summaries of cases on that topic can be found. To update this coverage, look under the same volume number, subject heading and paragraph numbers in the 'cumulative supplement'. This is reissued annually, and summarises cases decided since the publication date of the corresponding main volumes.

5.6.2 Using *Current Law* to find cases on a subject

Each paper *Current Law Year Book* (and *Monthly Digest*) includes a subject index. In theory, it is therefore possible to track cases on a subject, including summaries, by consulting each volume consecutively from 1947 onwards. This is clearly laborious, and not recommended! However, all of this content may be searched for the same purpose in one go using the subscription database *Westlaw*.

At the home page, enter one or more keywords in the 'Search by term(s)' box. Try to be as specific as possible. Click 'go'. A list of judgments whose summaries contain your keyword(s) appears in grey on the left of the screen. To view the *Current Law* summary of a listed case, click the blue number next to the party names.

5.6.3 Using full-text databases to find cases on a subject

Most full-text databases of case-law, such as Butterworths *All England Direct* or JUSTIS *Weekly Law Reports*, permit free-text subject searching using keywords. This is a thorough and powerful search facility.

However, it is important to understand the coverage of the database that you are using (for example, with *All England Direct*, you will find references to reports in a single series only, the *All England Reports*).

It is also important to understand the conventions of individual systems. The general principles of searching are constant. However, different publishers use different versions of search software. Therefore, using capital letters, or enclosing search terms in quotation marks, may generate very different results in two different databases. If in doubt, consult the on-screen help facility that most databases feature, or ask library staff for guidance.

Chapter 6

RESEARCHING LEGISLATION

6.1 INTRODUCTION

There are two classes of legislation in the UK:

- **primary legislation** is passed by Parliament, in the form of Acts (also known as statutes); around 50 are created each year;
- **secondary legislation** is made under powers delegated by Parliament, usually to government ministers; it almost always takes the form of statutory instruments (also known as regulations or orders); around 3,000 are created each year.

It is vital to check that the version of any legislation that you refer to is in force. Some provisions do not come into force for some time after they have been passed by Parliament. Many are amended over time, or even repealed altogether.

There are many different sources of legislation, in paper form and in electronic form. The first question to ask before you choose a source is this: do I need the original version of this provision, or do I need the version of the provision that is in force now? If you need the version in force now (ie incorporating any subsequent amendments and repeals), the best sources are probably *Halsbury's Statutes of England* (see **6.3.4**) or *Halsbury's Statutory Instruments* (see **6.5.2**). The electronic alternative is the subscription database *Legislation Direct* (see **6.6**).

6.2 CITATION

A statute is generally cited by its 'short title' (which should include the year it was passed): eg 'Human Rights Act 1998'. You may also come across citations by 'chapter number' (the first statute passed in a given year is chapter 1, and so on). Thus the Human Rights Act 1998 may be cited as 'c 42 1998' (because it was the forty-second Act to be passed in 1998). Since 1963, chapter numbering has followed the calendar year. Before 1963, chapter numbering related to the 'regnal year' during which the provision was passed by Parliament (where each regnal year began with the anniversary of the sovereign's accession to the throne). See any of the guides listed at the end of Chapter 2 for a full explanation of this complicated system.

A statutory instrument is cited in the form 'SI [year]/[serial number]': eg SI 1998/3132, which was the first published form of the Civil Procedure Rules 1998. The serial numbering reverts to '1' at the start of each calendar year.

6.3 SOURCES OF STATUTES

6.3.1 Official versions of Acts of Parliament

Upon receiving the Royal Assent, the official version of an Act is published by Her Majesty's Stationery Office (HMSO). It appears in paper form and also on the

HMSO website (see http://www.hmso.gov.uk/acts.htm). These texts are not subsequently amended. The paper versions are re-published each year as a series of hardback volumes entitled *Public General Acts and Measures*.

6.3.2 Current Law Statutes

Current Law Statutes publishes statutes chronologically. They first appear as looseleaf booklets. These are later re-published as several hardback volumes each year. This original version of the statute is then 'frozen' permanently: subsequent amendments and repeals are not incorporated. The editorial annotations are helpful (for example, references to parliamentary debates about the provision, as reported in *Hansard*).

6.3.3 Law Reports. Statutes series

Current Law Statutes first appeared in 1949. If you need to consult an older act as it was originally passed by Parliament, you may need to refer to the (confusingly titled!) *Law Reports. Statutes* series (1865–). Once again, the original version of the statute is 'frozen': any subsequent amendments and repeals are ignored.

6.3.4 Halsbury's Statutes of England

Halsbury's Statutes of England contains an annotated version of all statutes in force in England and Wales. Amendments are incorporated; repealed provisions are excluded. The arrangement is alphabetical by subject. It is the best source for consulting up-to-date versions of statutes.

To find out the law using the paper version of *Halsbury's Statutes of England*, you must take four steps:

- index;
- main volumes;
- cumulative supplement; and
- noter-up.

(a) Index

The paperback 'tables of statutes and consolidated index' contains an alphabetical and a chronological table of statutes, as well as a subject index. If you are uncertain of the provision that you need, think of subject terms that identify the problem you are researching. The subject index will refer you from these keywords to relevant statutes in a main volume:

> eg   **pharmaceutical services**
> accommodation, **30**, 845
> additional arrangements for providing, **30(S)**, NHS 145–6 …

The number in **bold** is the number of the volume in which the relevant statute appears. The following number in light type is the page number. If the reference is followed by **(S)**, the provision is a recent one and will be found in one of the 'current statutes service' looseleaf binders. The volume and subject arrangement of these is the same as the main set.

HOW TO USE *HALSBURY'S STATUTES*

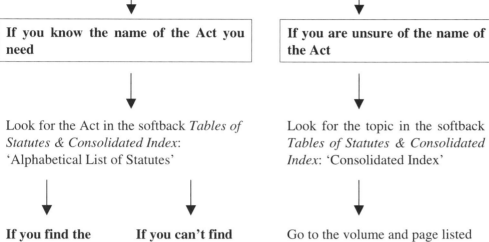

| If you know the name of the Act you need | If you are unsure of the name of the Act |

Look for the Act in the softback *Tables of Statutes & Consolidated Index*: 'Alphabetical List of Statutes'

Look for the topic in the softback *Tables of Statutes & Consolidated Index*: 'Consolidated Index'

If you find the Act, go to the volume and page listed (an 'S' in brackets means look in the *Current Statutes Service* binders)

If you can't find the Act, look in *Current Statutes Service*: binder A: 'Alphabetical List of Statutes' (includes Acts added to the Service since the latest *Tables of Statutes & Consolidated Index*)

Go to the volume and page listed (an 'S' in brackets means look in the *Current Statutes Service* binders)

IS THE INFORMATION STILL UP TO DATE?

Look in the annual hardback *Cumulative Supplement* for your volume and page number. An entry means the law has changed between the publication date of the volume and the operative date of the *Cumulative Supplement*.

Then look in the *Noter-up* binder for your volume and page number. An entry means the law has changed since the operative date of the *Cumulative Supplement*.

(b) Main volumes

The 50 'main volumes' feature statutes in force in England and Wales, arranged by subject. Volume 1 begins with admiralty. Volume 50 ends with wills. If a statute covers several subject areas, it may be split over several different volumes. The text is up to date to the year of publication of the volume (printed on the spine). Amended text appears in square brackets; text that has been repealed appears as '…'. Detailed footnotes provide useful commentary, including commencement information and sources of repeals and amendments.

(c) Cumulative supplement

Over the years, main volumes are re-issued on a rolling programme. Therefore you must always check whether the information in any main volume has changed since the volume's year of publication.

This updating process involves two stages. To begin with, consult the annual hardback 'cumulative supplement'. The content of this is up to date to at least the end of the year preceding its year of publication (the year of publication is printed on the spine). Any developments affecting your statute since publication of the main volumes are likely to feature here. Entries appear under the same volume and page references as in the main volumes.

(d) Noter-up

Finally, check the looseleaf 'noter-up' binder. This will alert you to any very recent changes in the law. Once again, look under the volume and page number of your original reference.

6.4 COMMENCEMENT OF STATUTES

A statute that has passed all its parliamentary stages and received Royal Assent may not necessarily come into effect straight away. To complicate matters further, often some sections of statutes enter into force before others. Sometimes sections are brought partially into effect, for a limited purpose and period, before entering fully into force later. And just occasionally a statute is repealed before it enters into force at all (eg Antarctic Minerals Act 1989)!

The last section of a statute usually deals with arrangements for its own commencement. A specific date may be given; a specific period after the date of Royal Assent may be stipulated; or the commencement may be delayed until such time as the Secretary of State makes a commencement order (usually by way of a statutory instrument). If no commencement statement is made within the text of a statute, you may assume that it came into force on the date of Royal Assent.

6.4.1 *Is it in Force?*

The paperback volume *Is it in Force?* is reissued annually as part of *Halsbury's Statutes of England*. It lists statutes passed in the preceding 25 years, with commencement details. Arrangement is by year, then alphabetical by title of statute, then by section. A supplement dealing with the current year appears in the looseleaf 'noter-up' binder of *Halsbury's Statutes of England*. The same content is also available as part of the subscription database *Legislation Direct* (see **6.6**): click the blue 'is it in force?' button on the home page for access.

*NB The title 'Is it in Force?' is misleading, in the sense that this publication covers commencement information only; it does not deal with amendments and repeals that may affect the status of your statute! For sources of information on amendments and repeals, see **6.7**.*

If your statute is more than 25 years old, you will need to consult the text of the provision itself for information about commencement. Alternatively, a practitioner book may give useful guidance.

6.5 SOURCES OF STATUTORY INSTRUMENTS

6.5.1 Official versions of statutory instruments

The official version of a statutory instrument is published by Her Majesty's Stationery Office (HMSO). It appears in paper form and also on the HMSO website (see http://www.hmso.gov.uk/stat.htm). These texts are not subsequently amended. The paper versions are re-published each year as a series of hardback volumes entitled *Statutory Instruments*.

6.5.2 *Halsbury's Statutory Instruments*

Halsbury's Statutory Instruments collects all statutory instruments in force in England and Wales. Many are reprinted in full; the remainder appear in summary. The arrangement is alphabetical by subject. It is the best source for discovering what relevant secondary legislation exists on a given topic.

To find out the law using the paper version of *Halsbury's Statutory Instruments*, you must take three steps:

- index;
- main volumes; and
- service binders.

(a) Index

The annual paperback 'consolidated index and alphabetical list of instruments' contains a subject index and a list of instruments by title. If you are uncertain of the title of the provision that you need, think of subject terms that identify the problem you are researching. The subject index will refer you from these 'keywords' to a main volume and a page.

If the reference in an index appears as '**(S)**' followed by a citation, the provision is a recent one and will be dealt with in the 'service' looseleaf binder.

(b) Main volumes

The 22 'main volumes' feature statutory instruments in force in England and Wales, arranged by subject. Volume 1 begins with agriculture. Volume 22 ends with wills. Each subject opens with a chronological contents list, and a list of relevant instruments no longer in force. The text is up to date to the year of publication of the volume (printed on the spine). Footnotes provide detailed commentary.

HOW TO USE *HALSBURY'S STATUTORY INSTRUMENTS*

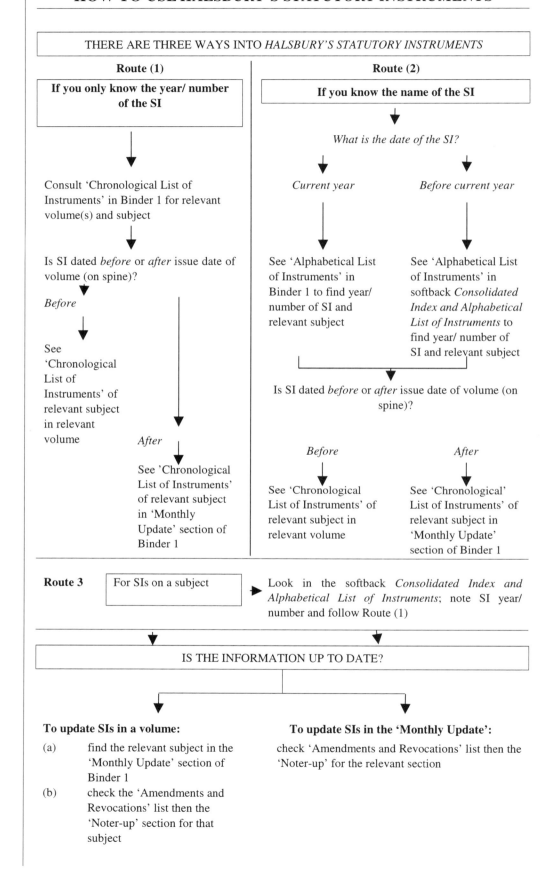

THERE ARE THREE WAYS INTO *HALSBURY'S STATUTORY INSTRUMENTS*

Route (1)

If you only know the year/ number of the SI

Consult 'Chronological List of Instruments' in Binder 1 for relevant volume(s) and subject

Is SI dated *before* or *after* issue date of volume (on spine)?

Before

See 'Chronological List of Instruments' of relevant subject in relevant volume

After

See 'Chronological List of Instruments' of relevant subject in 'Monthly Update' section of Binder 1

Route (2)

If you know the name of the SI

What is the date of the SI?

Current year

See 'Alphabetical List of Instruments' in Binder 1 to find year/ number of SI and relevant subject

Before current year

See 'Alphabetical List of Instruments' in softback *Consolidated Index and Alphabetical List of Instruments* to find year/ number of SI and relevant subject

Is SI dated *before* or *after* issue date of volume (on spine)?

Before

See 'Chronological List of Instruments' of relevant subject in relevant volume

After

See 'Chronological' List of Instruments' of relevant subject in 'Monthly Update' section of Binder 1

Route 3   For SIs on a subject   ▶ Look in the softback *Consolidated Index and Alphabetical List of Instruments*; note SI year/ number and follow Route (1)

IS THE INFORMATION UP TO DATE?

To update SIs in a volume:

(a)   find the relevant subject in the 'Monthly Update' section of Binder 1

(b)   check the 'Amendments and Revocations' list then the 'Noter-up' section for that subject

To update SIs in the 'Monthly Update':

check 'Amendments and Revocations' list then the 'Noter-up' for the relevant section

(c) Service binders

The 'main' looseleaf binder (no 1) contains a variety of indexing and updating tools. These include a 'chronological list of instruments', covering the whole publication and allowing you to find a provision where you only know its citation.

The largest section in the 'main' binder, the 'monthly update', lists changes to the statement of law given in the main volumes. Over the years, main volumes are re-issued on a rolling programme. Therefore you must always check whether the information in any main volume has changed since the volume's year of publication. Entries appear under the same volume and subject heading as in the main volumes. Check for any new provisions using the 'chronological list of instruments'. Then check for any changes to the effect of existing provisions using the list of 'revocations and amendments' and the subsequent 'noter-up'.

The 'additional texts' looseleaf binder (no 2) contains the full texts of selected recent instruments that will be incorporated in future editions of the main volumes.

6.6 *LEGISLATION DIRECT*

Scope

Legislation Direct features the full, amended texts of UK primary and secondary legislation in force. It is a Butterworths subscription database. (Butterworths also publishes the various *Halsbury's* encyclopedias in printed form.) Searching, especially by subject keyword, is fast and efficient.

Navigation

The front screen features on the right a broad-based search facility ('navigator'). On the left are direct links to separate parts of the database (including 'uk statutes' and 'uk si's'). This permits access by browsing, via contents lists, and also opens the way to more sophisticated search options.

The usual screen layout is split. The full text is on the right, appearing section by section. Amended text appears in square brackets; text that has been repealed appears as '...'. Footnotes provide brief details about commencements and sources of amending legislation. A contents list appears on the left, allowing you to jump to another provision (or section within a provision) at any time.

Searching

If you know the name or the citation of the provision that you need, use the 'navigator' search facility on the home page. Enter details in any of the boxes labelled 'full or partial title', 'series number', 'year'. Select 'type of enactment' from the drop-down list below. Click 'go'.

To search for references to a topic, select a sector of the database (eg statutes or statutory instruments) by clicking the appropriate button on the left of the home page. Point with the mouse to the blue 'search' link at the top of the screen. Click on the 'normal' option that appears. Enter the keyword(s) you wish to search for in the box at the top of the screen. If you enter more than one word, specify in the 'search how' box below whether these should appear 'next to each other in order' (ie as a phrase) or 'in any order in the same paragraph'. In the 'search where' box, click the button next to 'within current location'. Click 'go'.

'Stop press'

Legislation Direct is updated daily, in the sense that the content changes every day. However, that does not imply that the content is current up to today. Incorporating the effects of new legislation is a complex and time-consuming task. The 'stop-press' facility is intended to bridge the gap between the publisher becoming aware of new provisions, and those provisions being incorporated in the database. If you use 'stop press' properly, the publisher claims that your research will be up to date to within 2 days. (Even then, it is impossible to quote a precise date to which the law as stated is current!)

When consulting a provision, always check for any updates by clicking the blue 'stop press' link that appears in the top right of the screen. A separate window appears. Any new legislation that amends your provision, but whose effects have not yet been integrated throughout the database, will be listed. If the full text of the new provision has already been published on *Legislation Direct*, its title will appear as a blue hyperlink. Click the title to view the text.

6.7 UPDATING LEGISLATION

It is vital to check for changes to the legal status of legislation that you use in the course of your research. You need to consider two main agencies for such changes: subsequent amending legislation, and statements of interpretation by judges in subsequent cases.

The issue of amending legislation is especially critical if the source you have consulted is one that publishes provisions chronologically (for example, the HMSO website or *Current Law Statutes*). You can rely on *Halsbury's Statutes of England* and *Halsbury's Statutory Instruments* being current to within a few weeks, provided all the updating steps have been followed through properly. You can rely on *Legislation Direct* being up to date to within a few days, provided the 'stop press' facility has been consulted properly. However, it is always worthwhile double-checking for any amending legislation.

6.7.1 *Current Law Legislation Citator*

The *Current Law Legislation Citator* gives references to any subsequent legislation and cases that changed the legal status of a statute or a statutory instrument.

The printed version of the *Current Law Legislation Citator* comprises a series of hardback volumes, each covering a series of years, starting in 1947. These are supplemented by paperback volumes dealing with the most recent few years. The current year is covered by sections in the looseleaf *Current Law Statutes* 'service file'. Each volume is arranged chronologically by year, then provision number (chapter number for statutes or serial number for statutory instruments), then section number. The procedure is to find the earliest reference to your provision, then check the lists in subsequent volumes for later developments.

The same information is also available electronically as part of the *Westlaw* subscription database. At the home page, enter the name of the provision in the 'UK Legislation: Search by Name' box. Click 'go'. A list of search results (headed 'cite list') appears on the left of the screen. To view the text of a section, click the appropriate blue number from this list. Brief footnotes at the bottom of each section give the source of any amendments or repeals that have been incorporated in the text. While viewing the text, click the grey 'analysis' tab to see further references to developments in subsequent legislation (headed 'read with') and in subsequent cases (headed 'cases citing').

Chapter 7

RESEARCHING EUROPEAN COMMUNITY LAW

7.1 INTRODUCTION

Researching the law of the European Community (EC) requires skill and tenacity. The structure of the material is complex. The volume of new legislation and cases is large. There is often a significant time lag before developments filter into practitioner sources covering the state of UK law. Researchers who specialise in EC law become adept at using a variety of methods in their hunt for authority that may affect clients' business decisions. For example, telephoning an official department may yield timely and significant information that no standard source can offer.

This brief introduction to researching EC law aims to familiarise you with the key information sources. With some practice, you will be able to track down references to EC legislation and cases. You will also develop a feel for spotting possible 'Europoints' in a file, even if no such point seems to be in issue at first sight.

The authoritative text of EC law appears mainly in two bulky paper publications: the *Official Journal of the European Communities*, L-series, for legislation, and the *European Court Reports* for case-law. Printed alternatives from commercial publishers are more widespread and easier to use. The EC itself also publishes a vast amount of information, including primary legal materials, on the internet.

7.2 GENERAL SOURCES

7.2.1 *European Current Law*

European Current Law allows you to trace developments over time. Monthly parts summarise legislation and case-law. They include tables and indexes that accumulate throughout the year. All material is subsequently republished as a bound 'year book'.

7.2.2 Vaughan *Law of the European Communities*

This encyclopedia is published in four looseleaf volumes. It gives commentary on the whole of EC law, under 23 subject headings. Separate tables and indexes appear for each subject section. If you need a general explanation of an area of EC law before researching primary sources, this is a good starting point.

7.3 PRIMARY LEGISLATION

The primary legislation of the EC comprises the founding Treaties that established the three European Communities, along with later amending treaties (most recently the Treaty of Nice (signed 2001)). These documents lay out the aspirations and objectives of the Community. The accession treaties that admit new Member States also fall under the heading of primary legislation.

The official text of the treaties may be freely accessed via the EC website, 'Europa' (see http://europa.eu.int/eur-lex/en/treaties/dat/EC_consol.html). Various paper sources reprint the treaties. These include the looseleaf *Encyclopedia of European Union Law: Constitutional Texts*, and the annual student text, *Blackstone's EC Legislation*.

7.4 SECONDARY LEGISLATION

7.4.1 Introduction

The secondary legislation of the EC sets out how the objectives expressed in the treaties are to be accomplished. Various types of provision fall under this heading:

- Regulations (directly applicable in Member States: no need for national legislation);
- Directives (Member States must legislate to implement within a fixed period);
- Decisions (addressed to particular Member States, companies or individuals);
- Recommendations and Opinions (non-binding suggestions for action).

In practice, you will mainly encounter Regulations and Directives. Citations for these can be confusing. A Regulation is cited by running number then year (ie 1/99 is the first Regulation of 1999); a Directive is cited by year then running number (ie 99/1 is the first Directive of 1999).

7.4.2 Sources of EC Secondary Legislation

(1) CELEX

The most reliable electronic source for the full text of all secondary legislation is the subscription database *CELEX*. This is the official legal database of the European Commission. It is available direct from the EC. However, access is more commonly through other commercial channels such as *LEXIS* (published by Butterworths) or *JUSTIS* (published by Context). The content of *CELEX* is awkward to search and navigate, but on-screen help facilities are always available.

(2) EUR-Lex

An EC project to consolidate this large body of legislation for free publication on the internet is ongoing (see http://europa.eu.int/eur-lex/en/lif/index.html). It is called EUR-Lex, and describes itself as, '... consolidated texts, that is, *non-official* documents which integrate a basic instrument of Community legislation with its subsequent amendments and corrections in a single text'. The database may be browsed by subject or searched by keyword.

EUR-Lex also offers access to a growing archive of issues of the *Official Journal*. At the time of writing, all issues from 1 January 1998 are available.

(3) Encyclopedia of European Community Law: Volume C

A selective paper source for secondary legislation in force is the looseleaf *Encyclopedia of European Community Law: Volume C: Community Secondary Legislation*. There are 11 binders (the numbers on the spines are in Roman numerals!). Legislation is arranged by subject (indicated by plastic dividers), then chronologically within each subject. Look in the 'service information and release bulletin' section, at the front of binder I, for an indication of the currency of the law as stated.

If you have the citation for a provision, look it up in one of the contents tables at the front of binder I. Otherwise consult the two subject indexes at the back of binder XI (the second is a 'supplementary index', covering the most recent additions). Both will refer you to a numbered section beginning with 'C' (corresponding to the subject dividers within the binders) and a paragraph number. For example, if you look up Directive 99/32, you are referred to C8-614. This provision will be found in Part C8 ('Fuel and Power'), beginning at paragraph 614.

7.4.3 How to check if EC legislation is still in force

EC secondary legislation is subject to later amendments and repeals. There are several ways of tracing the current status of a given provision.

The EC publishes an authoritative two-volume *Directory of Community Legislation in Force* twice each year. Volume 2 contains a numerical and an alphabetical index to volume 1, which gives details of current status. The same content is also available via the EUR-Lex website. However, the information is awkward to use in both formats.

Butterworths' *European Communities Legislation: Current Status* is the most efficient paper source. It is published in two annual volumes, updated by quarterly supplements. Provisions are listed by year, then by reference number, with details of whether they are still in force. There is a separate subject index volume.

CELEX gives details of amendments and repeals in relation to pieces of secondary legislation. Alternatively, search for the provision via the 'legislation in force' section of the EUR-Lex website. If the provision is not found, it is not in force. If it is found, amendments will be listed, with links to the amending instruments.

7.4.4 How to check if an EC Directive has entered into force in the UK

The paperback *Butterworths EC Legislation Implementator* is published twice a year. It lists EC Directives that have been incorporated into UK law, along with references to implementing provisions (usually statutory instruments). Arrangement is alphabetical by Directive number.

CELEX includes details of national implementation in relation to EC Directives.

A possible electronic alternative to establish whether a Directive has been brought into force is to search a full text database of UK legislation. Use the Directive number as your search term. Start with statutory instruments, since implementation is usually effected by this method. Move on to statutes if this is unsuccessful.

7.4.5 Proposed legislation

It is important to be alert to proposed legislation when researching the European dimension of a problem. However, draft EC legislation is notoriously difficult to trace. It can take several years to agree the final version of a provision. Final drafts are published as COM documents (also known as 'COM docs'), this being the title of a range of working documents of the European Commission. They are cited in the form: **COM** (*year*) *running number*, **final**. Final drafts also appear in the *Official Journal*, C-series (Information and Notices), published in paper and electronic form.

Several commercial current awareness services are intended to alert subscribers to proposed EC legislation. These include *Butterworths EC Brief* in paper form, and the 'EU Daily Update' service from the subscription database *Lawtel*.

As a last resort, advice can be obtained by contacting the offices of the European Commission Representation in the UK (see http://www.cec.org.uk for details).

7.5 CASE-LAW

7.5.1 Introduction

EC cases are heard before either the Court of Justice or the Court of First Instance. The latter was inaugurated in 1989, with the aim of lessening the load on the Court of Justice by dealing with certain categories of dispute.

The UK practitioner will be unaccustomed to certain aspects of the procedure of EC courts:

- judgments are preceded by an 'opinion' of the Advocate-General; this is not necessarily binding on the court, but its reasoning is usually followed;
- applications to the court that concern the same area of law may be joined together;
- the names of parties are often very long; some leading cases are therefore referred to by popular abbreviations, which may or may not appear in electronic databases or indexes to paper sources!
- the court delivers one judgment only: there are no dissenting opinions.

7.5.2 Citation

The case number is an important feature of any case heard by the European Court of Justice. A full citation gives the case number first, followed by the parties, then the citation of the authoritative report in the paper version of the *European Court Reports*. For example:

> C-295/95 *Farrell v Long* [1997] ECR I-1683

The case number comprises a running serial number followed by the year of application or reference to the Court (note that application and judgment may be separated by several years!). Since the creation of the Court of First Instance in 1989, all cases are prefixed by 'C-' (Court of Justice, or 'Cour' in French) or 'T-' (Court of First Instance, or 'Tribunal' in French).

7.5.3 Sources of EC Cases

The bare texts of judgments of the European Court of Justice since June 1997 are freely available via the 'Europa' website (see http://europa.eu.int/cj/en/index.htm). Some libraries also collect paper versions of these transcripts.

CELEX contains the full text of judgments delivered since the Court was founded. It is the most effective source for searching for cases by party name, case number or subject.

Judgments are subsequently checked, translated into all EC languages and re-published in the *European Court Reports*. The opinion of the Advocate General is also included. The paper version of this series is officially the authoritative source for EC case-law. However, publication may involve delay of a year or more. The full text is also available via the subscription databases *Westlaw* and *LEXIS*.

Common Market Law Reports is the more timely (but unofficial) alternative to the *European Court Reports*. All significant EC cases are included, as well as selected decisions of Member State national courts. The paper version appears in five volumes each year (vols 4 and 5 deal with antitrust materials). It is indexed by subject, by case party and by case number. The full text is also available via the subscription database *Westlaw*.

The Digest may be used to trace the full citation of leading EC cases, and to search for cases on a subject.

Chapter 8

THE RESULTS OF LEGAL RESEARCH

8.1 RECORDING THE RESEARCH

It is tempting not to make any notes at all when researching a problem, and rely instead on memory. This is not a wise approach, even if it appears that only a quick answer is wanted. Often the true value of a piece of information becomes clear only at the end of a research trail: accurate references will then save time. And what if your principal questions the answer? What about if s/he wants you to check back on something, or wants to know the steps you took to reach your answer?

As well as recording the information you discover, always jot down notes about the following as you research:

* titles of the sources consulted;
* keywords used during searches;
* page references for key pieces of information;
* dates of publication (including the date of the latest release for a looseleaf source);
* date to which the law as stated is claimed to be up to date by the publisher;
* date your research was carried out (especially important with internet sources, where content may change daily).

8.2 REPORTING RESEARCH

If your research is carried out at the request of your principal, it is important that you communicate the results clearly. In any event, it is as well to make a clear record of the legal basis for advice.

Reports in practice will take different forms, depending on the purpose and importance of the research, and whether the researcher understands the client's position fully. As a trainee you are likely to begin with relatively simple tasks, so that a relatively simple form of report will suffice. Suggestions for the content of more elaborate forms of reports, together with useful advice on style and layout, will be found in Chapter 1 (*Writing and Drafting*).

The following general points should be borne in mind:

* the main aims of the report are to answer the question clearly, including enough detail of the research for sources to be traced and for conclusions to be checked easily;
* begin by restating the problem; if you have a different view of the problem from your principal, you are unlikely to produce a satisfactory answer;
* include a brief summary of your conclusions near the beginning of the report, separately from any reasoning or source references, so that the main message is quickly apparent;

- if your problem is complex, involving several linked issues, list the issues and report on each one separately;
- consider the recipient of the research in making choices about style and layout: Is it appropriate to report results in note form? Is it reasonable to assume knowledge of the legal background? Will technical language be easily understood?
- if the factual context is known, the results should be applied to the facts, and brief notes should be made of obvious practical implications;
- give full source references; include the title and citation of primary sources, and the page/paragraph numbers of the publications where they were found;
- consider attaching a photocopy/print-out of the most relevant sources;
- state what steps were taken to update; give the date of the latest sources used, and also give (where possible) the date to which the law as stated is claimed to be up to date by the publisher;
- state the date that the research was carried out;
- state the date that the report was compiled.

PART III

ORAL COMMUNICATION SKILLS

Chapter 9

INTRODUCTION TO ORAL COMMUNICATION SKILLS

9.1 GENERAL

'One-third of what is said is not heard

One-third is heard but not understood

One-third is understood – but may not be accepted'

(adapted from a passage in *The Skills of Negotiating* by Bill Scott)

All solicitors need to possess good oral communication skills in order to defeat the 'one-third rule', quoted above, and to become effective interviewers, negotiators or advocates.

Solicitors also need to establish and maintain good working relationships with their colleagues in the office (whether professional or administrative), with members of other professions whom they have to consult or instruct, and with representatives of official bodies (eg court staff).

Although oral communication skills are largely based on common sense, people's ability to use them varies enormously. Some people are naturally better than others, but everyone is capable of improvement. Like any other skill (driving a car, playing a musical instrument, playing a sport), performance can be improved by learning specific skills and techniques, and then practising them.

At first, practising new techniques can feel artificial ('It's just not me') but after a while the technique usually becomes second nature (like changing gear in a car). However, skills training should not be allowed to suppress natural ability, and it is possible to be a competent interviewer, negotiator or advocate without necessarily having to perform every technique by the book. It is a question of balance; but success comes through practising sound techniques. Brilliant mavericks are rare.

This chapter introduces those aspects of oral communication skills which are common to interviewing, negotiation and advocacy. Chapters 10–12 explain how the skills apply to each of these activities.

9.2 LISTENING

In order to advise a client, or to persuade an opponent or the court, solicitors have first to *demonstrate* that they have both heard and understood what the other has said.

This involves listening carefully to what is being said. However, listening is an underrated skill which requires considerable concentration. Listening as a solicitor is very different from listening in the context of ordinary social discourse, where interchanges are shorter and more fluid and where there is less need to pick up every nuance or recall precisely what was said. Listening as a solicitor is also different from listening to lectures, where students do not necessarily have to interrelate with the lecturer and may be able to copy up notes from elsewhere later. Nevertheless, students who are good listeners in lectures will find that this skill will help them enormously in practice.

Most authorities on oral communication skills make a distinction between 'passive listening' and 'active listening'.

9.2.1 Passive listening

Passive listening involves using silences and other unobtrusive signals to encourage the speaker to continue. For example, when interviewing, negotiating or conducting advocacy, the solicitor might want to induce the speaker to carry on speaking and thereby perhaps volunteer a crucial piece of information.

Silences can be embarrassing in normal social situations, so many people learn during their upbringing to avoid them. Yet silence is one of the most powerful techniques available to a solicitor. It may require a conscious effort to remain silent for longer than normal in the hope that the speaker will fill the void with more information.

Other non-obtrusive signals a solicitor may give the speaker to encourage him to continue include:

- eye contact;
- posture;
- nodding;
- acknowledgments ('Uh, huh');
- express invitations ('Go on').

9.2.2 Active listening

Active listening, as the phrase suggests, involves more obtrusive techniques which demonstrate to the other person that the solicitor has both heard and understood.

The most common form of active listening is summarising (ie giving a short, clear precis of what the speaker has just said). Like silence, the technique is not regularly employed in social conversations and so requires a conscious effort.

Summarising is also used by solicitors to check the effectiveness of communication in the reverse direction (ie that the other person has heard and understood the solicitor).

9.3 QUESTIONING

Questioning skills are well-known tools of the solicitor's trade. Questions can be classified according to the breadth of the response they allow (ie as open or closed questions).

9.3.1 Open questions

Open questions give maximum freedom to the person being questioned, they encourage expansion, and they do not seek to influence the content of the reply.

> *Examples*
> 'So what happened next?'
>
> 'What were your reactions to that?'
>
> 'How did you respond to the offer?'
>
> 'Why did you do that?'
>
> 'Tell me about your relationship with the managing director.'
>
> 'Tell me more about …'

Open questions do not necessarily have to be worded as questions: 'Tell me …' is a phrase which can be used to invite an open response.

9.3.2 Closed questions

Closed questions invite a narrow answer, from a few words or a sentence to a 'Yes'/'No' reply (sometimes called 'Yes/No questions').

> *Examples*
> 'Were you also carrying a knife?'
>
> 'Did you accept the offer?'

One particular form of closed question is the leading question. For example, the questioner might deliberately seek to influence the content of the reply by asking a question which encourages a particular answer 'So you must have been drunk, mustn't you?'

9.4 NON-VERBAL COMMUNICATION

Non-verbal communication includes eye contact, posture and gestures and is often called 'body language'.

Careful observation of the body language of other people can provide clues as to how they are feeling, or how they are responding to advice or to an argument, and can therefore be influential in deciding how to proceed. However, tread cautiously, because the clue might not be conclusive: the interpretation of body language is controversial, and is subject to cultural variations. Be aware of non-verbal communication, but do not allow it to distract you from everything else.

Similarly, awareness of how your own body language affects both yourself and others can help in deciding how to convey your message more effectively. Although it is sometimes said that one cannot (or should not) 'fake' body language, cause and effect are often interrelated. Sitting with your arms tightly folded and your legs crossed, or nervously drumming your fingers or tapping your foot, can affect your own feelings as well as influencing others' perceptions of you. Sitting or standing in a physically relaxed manner can help you feel more relaxed.

A useful book is *Body Language* by Allan Pease (Sheldon Press).

Chapter 10

INTERVIEWING AND ADVISING

10.1 OBJECTIVES OF A SOLICITOR/CLIENT INTERVIEW

This chapter concentrates on the skills needed during the first interview with a client. There are four main objectives:

(1) to establish good **rapport** between the solicitor and the client;
(2) to obtain relevant **information** from the client;
(3) to help the client reach appropriate **decisions**;
(4) to plan future **action**.

Other legal interviews (eg with witnesses) usually serve more limited purposes.

10.2 COMMON FAILINGS

There are many reasons why a solicitor may fail to achieve the above objectives.

For example, the solicitor may:

- fail to listen properly;
- talk too much;
- make a premature diagnosis;
- restrict the areas in which the client feels free to talk;
- be over-directive in suggesting what further action is necessary.

The skills referred to later in this chapter will reduce the likelihood of any of these failings occuring.

10.3 TWO INGREDIENTS FOR SUCCESS – SKILLS AND STRUCTURE

10.3.1 Skills

In order to achieve the objectives referred to in **10.1**, a solicitor needs to make effective use of a wide range of skills.

The principal skills involved are:

(1) **listening**;
(2) **questioning**;
(3) **analysing**;
(4) **explaining**;
(5) **note-taking**.

These will be considered in more detail in **10.4**.

10.3.2 Structure

The objectives in **10.1** are easier to achieve if the solicitor prepares for and conducts the interview in a logical and coherent manner.

Structure and management involve:

(1)   creating a **suitable environment** for the interview;
(2)   **preparing adequately** for the interview;
(3)   using an **appropriate 'model'** for the interview itself.

A 'model' is merely a predetermined structure, under which the interview is divided into a logical sequence of stages. Each stage involves the performance of essential tasks and requires the use of different combinations of the skills referred to above.

The model used in this book is:

GREETING

(1)   PRELIMINARIES
(2)   OBTAINING THE FACTS
(3)   FILLING IN THE DETAIL
(4)   ADVISING
(5)   CLOSING

PARTING

The model is easy to follow and can be used in any legal context, although the length of time spent on each stage will usually vary depending on whether the interview is litigation or transaction based.

A detailed explanation of these stages will be given at **10.5** but a brief overview of the three central stages will help your understanding of what follows in **10.4** about the relevant skills. Thus:

Obtaining the facts

Involves the client giving an account of the matter with as little interruption from the solicitor as possible. It is therefore characterised by the client talking and the solicitor **listening** and encouraging the client to continue.

Filling in the detail

Involves a more active role by the solicitor to ensure that a complete and accurate picture is obtained and recorded. This stage is therefore characterised by the solicitor **questioning** the client and taking notes of what the client says.

Advising

Involves supplying the information which the client needs in order to make necessary decisions and to give the solicitor instructions for any further action. This stage therefore usually takes the form of the solicitor analysing and **explaining** the client's position, explaining the range of options open to the client and then **engaging in a dialogue** to make necessary decisions and to agree a plan of action.

10.4 THE SKILLS

10.4.1 Listening – an undervalued skill

Encouraging a client to tell his/her own story is generally a more effective way of gathering information than attempting to do so by a series of closed questions. You should therefore avoid asking questions until you have a reasonably full version of the case.

If the client is verbose, you may need to adopt a more forceful braking role, but this should occur only when absolutely necessary.

Listening is an undervalued skill which involves a range of techniques to sustain information-giving.

Silence

In everyday conversation, periods of silence can sometimes seem awkward and even cause embarrassment.

In an interview, these periods give the client time to think, tell the story as he/she remembers it, and express the feelings it creates.

You must therefore learn to control the natural urge to fill silences.

Body language

Consider how your body language may help or hinder building good rapport with the client. For example:

(1) eye contact: a friendly, but not a prolonged stare;
(2) posture: leaning slightly towards the client;
(3) head-nodding: but not too much;
(4) avoiding irritating/distracting mannerisms, eg pen-tapping, foot-drumming, etc.

Acknowledgments

Brief indications (without interrupting) showing attention, interest, and under-standing, such as:

> 'Yes, I see'

> '… in Brussels?'

> 'Mhmmmm'.

Invitations to continue/elaborate

Examples are:

> 'Go on'

> 'What happened?'

> 'Tell me more about that'.

Reflecting feeling

This involves making it clear that you understand how the client feels; for example: 'I can quite see why you feel so angry about this' or (in relation to bereavement) 'I'm sorry to hear that'.

It involves expressing empathy with the client's feelings; not being judgmental about them.

The technique is useful in building rapport and is particularly important where the client's emotions will be a major factor in the case, for example in matrimonial cases or where the client has recently been bereaved.

However, reflecting feeling may also be appropriate in interviews which may appear to be less personal, for example when a commercial client has anxieties about losing face within the company if a transaction fails to reach a satisfactory conclusion.

You can gain valuable insights into the client's feelings by observing and correctly interpreting the client's body language, not merely from listening to the client's words and tone of voice.

10.4.2 Questioning

In an initial interview, a solicitor needs to obtain information on:

(1)   the nature of the client's problem or proposed transaction;
(2)   the relevant background facts;
(3)   the client's feelings and objectives.

Whilst much of this may be obtained through use of the listening techniques discussed above, it will usually be necessary to clarify and probe further by questioning.

For an initial interview, particularly in the early stages, open questions usually have more advantages than closed questions and failure to recognise this leads many interviews into an interviewer-dominated style. It is important to avoid asking more than one question at a time.

(1) Open questions

The advantages of open questions are that they:

* allow the client to select the subject-matter;
* allow the client to select the information the client believes to be relevant;
* allow the client to start with information about which the client feels comfortable;
* enable the client to get things 'off his chest';
* give the client freedom to reflect and to feel more actively involved in the interview;
* encourage memory by association, which may produce information which would be overlooked if the client were asked only closed questions.

The disadvantages are that they:

* may initially produce insufficient information;
* may encourage the client to verbosity and/or irrelevance;
* may inhibit a reticent client.

(2) Closed questions

The advantages of closed questions are that they:

* are a good method of obtaining precise details;
* may guide a client less stressfully through a sensitive area;

- may give confidence to an initially reticent or anxious client;
- may help to prompt memory;
- help to clarify and probe areas of ambiguity or uncertainty;
- may quieten a verbose client.

The disadvantages are that they:

- may lead to an over-clinical or 'processing' style of interview;
- may deprive the client of the opportunity to state the case in his own words;
- may inhibit rapport;
- reduce the opportunity to listen to and observe the client, and to understand his needs;
- may lead the solicitor to miss important areas of information because the client is not allowed to associate ideas freely;
- may even result in the solicitor directing the interview down a totally irrelevant path.

(3) The 'T-funnel'

The use of open questions followed by closed questions is sometimes known as the T-funnel sequence of questioning:

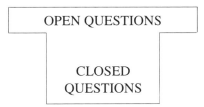

The solicitor introduces a particular topic with a series of open questions. Only after the open questions cease to be productive should they be narrowed into closed questions.

Premature use of closed questions may distort the response or lead to important details being omitted.

Example

(Open questions)

Solicitor	'What happened next?'
Client	'I got out of my car.'
Solicitor	'Yes ...?'
Client	'Well, I went over to where he'd parked his car and spoke to him.'

(Closed questions)

Solicitor	'Could you tell me exactly where you were both standing and exactly what was said?'
Client	'Yes, he was standing by the offside front wing of his car and as I approached him I am afraid I told him what I thought of him.'
Solicitor	'Can you remember the words you actually used?'
Client	'I said "You're a ***** – why the hell didn't you indicate?"'
Solicitor	'Did he reply?'

Client	'Yes, he said "I'm sorry – I didn't realise they'd changed the lane markings."'
Solicitor	'Anything else?'
Client	'No.'
Solicitor	'Was anyone else present?'
Client	'Yes – his wife was standing right next to him.'

(4) Further clarification and probing

It will often be necessary to probe further:

- to resolve remaining areas of ambiguity;
- to jog the client's memory;
- to clarify client needs and reaction to consequences of action;
- to discover how the client will respond to the legal process (in litigation) or to a counter-argument or proposal (negotiating a transaction).

The following are some techniques to achieve these objectives.

GOING BACK ONE STAGE

This involves taking the client back one stage in the narrative and inviting the client to relive the sequence of events in order to jog the memory:

> 'Take me through that again but starting from before you were approaching the road junction.'

This technique is useful, as it encourages the client to fill in any gaps in the narrative.

LEADING QUESTIONS

Leading questions can be a useful way of helping clients to convey something which they may have difficulty in articulating in their own words:

> 'So you've had disagreements with the managing director before?'

> 'So sexual intercourse did take place on that occasion?'

PREFACING A QUESTION WITH EXPLANATION

This can counteract the client perceiving your question as irrelevant or allay the client's anxiety in a sensitive area. For example:

> 'I know you're very confident of being acquitted but, if you are convicted, the magistrates will sentence you immediately. For that reason I now need to ask you some questions about your financial circumstances.'

There is, however, a danger that the explanation may influence (and therefore distort) the client's reply.

CROSS-CHECKING

This is often necessary where the information given by the client reveals gaps or contradictions which require explanation. For example:

> 'Are you quite sure about that because according to the police report you said you'd drunk three pints?'

DEVIL'S ADVOCATE

To play devil's advocate is to suggest to the client a different and adverse interpretation of his story. For example:

> 'If you're so sure that the accident wasn't your fault, why did you say to the other motorist: "I'm sorry – I just didn't see you coming"?'

It is generally advisable to explain why you are doing this because, otherwise, your apparent hostility is likely to damage rapport. For example:

> 'I'm sorry to ask you so bluntly but it's a question you are bound to be asked in court if this gets to trial.'

CHECKLISTS

Some interviews lend themselves to the use of checklists.

Used appropriately, a checklist has the obvious advantage that essential information is unlikely to be overlooked. A checklist also provides you with a concise and convenient source of information for speedy future reference.

However, interviewing a client simply by running through a checklist, particularly at the beginning of the interview, may inhibit effective communication. You may appear to be merely 'processing a case' rather than listening to the client's unique personal problem. Using a checklist in such a manner may damage rapport. The client may get a feeling of not being listened to if your questions jump from one topic to another rather than following up on the client's current train of thought.

Indeed, premature use of a checklist (ie before a correct diagnosis of the problem has been made) can waste valuable time while a mass of irrelevant information is accumulated. In other words, make quite sure that your chosen checklist is appropriate before using it!

(5) Summarising

This is an extremely important and useful technique.

Its purpose is to double check that your understanding of the facts and of your client's feelings and concerns is correct.

A summary of the key facts should be given at the end of the filling in the detail stage and before moving into the advising stage:

> 'OK, now before we talk about what needs to be done let me just check with you that I have got a correct and complete list of all your relevant assets.'

Apart from giving the client an opportunity to correct errors and supply additional facts, summarising reassures the client that you have heard and understood what you have been told. It also gives you a useful breathing space to think about the matter and the advice that needs to be given. It may also identify some areas on which further questioning is needed before you can safely advise.

Remember that summarising your understanding of the client's feelings and objectives is just as important as summarising factual information:

> 'So let me see whether I've correctly understood what you are hoping to achieve out of all this ...'

> 'So would it be fair to say that you would only be prepared to go to court if Janice's name could be kept out of it?'

Summarising helps you to identify when further questions need to be asked and what advice to give.

10.4.3 Analysing

Once the facts and the client's goals have been identified, the solicitor must (at least mentally) analyse which facts and legal principles are relevant, how the law applies to those facts and so reach a conclusion about the client's position and the range of available courses of action.

This process is familiar even to an inexperienced solicitor because it involves essentially the same techniques needed to answer traditional problem-solving questions in law examinations.

One obvious difference is that in real life the solicitor has to elicit the relevant information rather than having it spoon-fed in the form of a given scenario. Another difference is that the solicitor has little or no time for quiet reflection before being expected to offer at least a tentative view of the position.

What tends to happen in most interviews is that, at quite an early stage, the solicitor starts to form a provisional theory about the likely end position. This inevitably has to be reviewed and modified as additional information emerges and the solicitor must be careful to avoid reaching a conclusion until all the facts have been obtained.

Like all skills, this process becomes easier with experience, practice and greater familiarity with the law in question.

Listening, questioning, note-taking and trying to formulate advice cannot be tackled simultaneously – just one reason why it is helpful to build in periods of 'thinking time' as discussed in **10.4.2***(5)* above.

10.4.4 Explaining

Once you have analysed the client's position, a number of matters will usually have to be explained before the client can be expected to make decisions and give instructions.

This frequently involves explaining concepts which will be second nature to you and which you would normally express in legal terminology (such as 'consideration' or 'implied conditions/warranties' etc).

It is therefore easy to overlook the simple fact that concepts and terminology which seem quite straightforward and normal to you can be totally bewildering and meaningless to a lay client.

Clarity is vital and legal jargon should therefore be avoided at all costs. You must bear constantly in mind that **accurate and faultlessly reasoned advice is utterly useless to a client who cannot understand it**. It is true to say that, with practice and experience, you will learn your own way of expressing legal concepts in ways that clients will understand.

You should also bear in mind that, even when you have explained matters clearly, it is often unrealistic to expect the client to remember everything once the interview is over. For this reason it is desirable in most cases to send a follow-up letter to the client summarising the advice which you have given.

It is often helpful to ask the client whether what you have said has been understood and offer to repeat the advice. If overdone, this technique may appear patronising. If used appropriately, even the most self-confident client will appreciate your concern and a more timid client, who may be reluctant to ask directly, will welcome a genuine offer of clarification.

10.4.5 Note-taking

Note-taking is an important and difficult skill.

No solicitor can memorise every piece of information on all his/her files and there may be occasions when some other member of the firm will need to take over the file permanently or temporarily.

The file must therefore contain a complete, accurate and legible record of the interview.

This is best achieved by taking manuscript notes during the interview itself and, if necessary, having a fuller and/or clearer version typed afterwards.

Failing to take notes during the interview and intending to dictate everything immediately after the interview is fraught with danger because you may unavoidably become involved in other distractions and be unable to do this before memory has faded. The longhand notes must, at minimum, be sufficient to operate as an aide memoire of the vital facts, dates, assets, etc from which a fuller record can later be prepared.

Difficulties can arise if you try to take detailed notes too early in the interview, while the client is trying to tell his/her story. If you write while the client is actually talking, this can damage rapport for two reasons. First, it is very difficult to follow the meaning of what the client is saying if you are frantically trying to translate it into a written note. Secondly, it is impossible to write at length without losing eye contact with the client. Few things are more off-putting for a client than trying to relate a story to the top of someone's head! On the other hand, it can be equally off-putting if you interrupt the flow of the client's narrative by requesting time to write everything down.

The solution is simple. **Do not attempt to take notes during the obtaining the facts stage**; instead, concentrate on listening to the client's version of events and defer taking notes until the 'filling in the detail' stage. This may mean that you have to ask the client to repeat some matters but is likely to be less time consuming in the long run. Alternatively, restrict note-taking to very brief jottings which do not destroy eye contact but which will serve at a later stage as reminders of topics which need to be expanded.

Even when fuller note-taking starts, try to develop a concise style and be selective about what you write down. Headings can be used effectively to give a structure to your notes. Ensure that key names, addresses, figures, dates and verbatim accounts of conversations are accurately worded. Never be embarrassed to ask the client for the correct spellings if names are unfamiliar.

10.5 STRUCTURE AND MANAGEMENT

10.5.1 Before the interview

The environment

It is important that the interview should take place in an environment which will help rather than hinder effective communication. The aim should be to create an atmosphere in which the client will feel calm and relaxed and which will give a favourable impression of you and your firm.

You should therefore ensure:

(1) that the client will be physically comfortable;
(2) that the interview will be free from unnecessary interruptions;
(3) that the office surroundings convey a sense of well-organised professionalism without being austere and/or impersonal.

Seating arrangements may also help or hinder effective communication. Views on this topic differ and an arrangement which seems friendly and welcoming to one client may strike another as over-familiar or even invasive.

However, as far as possible, the arrangement should be one in which:

(1) the solicitor and client can clearly see and hear each other;
(2) the client does not feel kept at a distance at one extreme or invaded at the other;
(3) the solicitor and (if necessary) the client can make written notes in comfort.

The traditional arrangement in which the solicitor and client face each other from opposite sides of the solicitor's desk will usually satisfy the above criteria, provided the desk is not piled high with files and papers. It is also the arrangement which most clients will be expecting.

However, depending on the personality of the client and the nature of the matter, you may decide that a less formal arrangement, perhaps without the intervening desk, would be more relaxing for the client and therefore more conducive to communication.

Furthermore, there may be occasions (eg where the client needs to explain a plan, diagram or map to the solicitor) when sitting alongside the client is the only effective arrangement.

You should therefore consider the possibility of other arrangements and adopt them whenever appropriate.

The above comments presuppose that the interview will take place in an environment over which you have some degree of control, but the interview may, for a variety of reasons, take place in surroundings (eg hospital ward, prison cell, crowded court corridor, etc) over which you will have little or no control.

Preparing for the interview

Where possible/appropriate, you should:

(1) carry out a 'conflict check' to ensure that taking instructions from any new client will not give rise to a conflict of interest with any existing clients;
(2) in the case of a new client, ensure the client is aware of the need to provide the firm with proof of identity in cases where the Money Laundering Regulations 1993 apply;

(3) obtain background information on the client (and, where relevant, the client's business);

(4) request relevant documents and consider them in advance;

(5) research the relevant area of law, being careful not to pre-judge the issues or 'pigeon-hole' the client;

(6) make a checklist;

(7) ensure that the interview will be free from interruptions (especially the telephone).

10.5.2 The model

GREETING

(1)   PRELIMINARIES
(2)   OBTAINING THE FACTS
(3)   FILLING IN THE DETAIL
(4)   ADVISING
(5)   CLOSING

PARTING

What now follows is a step-by-step account of each successive stage in the model, indicating the purpose of each stage and which skills need to be employed.

10.5.3 Greeting

The importance of a warm and friendly greeting cannot be over-emphasised.

When you are ready to see the client, either go yourself to the reception area and escort the client to where the interview will take place, or make sure that some other member of staff does so. A client who is left to find his/her own way to your office through a bewildering maze of corridors is unlikely to arrive feeling welcome.

The client will form an impression of you immediately you meet. You should therefore do everything possible to ensure that this impression is favourable and that the client is made to feel welcome, comfortable and relaxed.

Greet the client by shaking hands, making eye contact and addressing the client by name. You should also introduce yourself by name and explain your status within the firm (eg trainee solicitor, solicitor, partner, etc).

The above points are simply common courtesy and may seem obvious, but they are extremely important.

After greeting, it is a matter of judgement how quickly you proceed to the business at hand, but most clients will have been rehearsing what they wish to say and will be ready to begin at once.

10.5.4 Preliminaries

In most cases, the client will have given some indication of the general nature of the problem and the reason for seeking advice when arranging the appointment for the interview.

Indeed, it is important to train secretaries and administrative staff who arrange appointments to make suitable enquiries to ensure that the client sees a solicitor whose expertise is appropriate to the matter in question.

Nevertheless, ambiguities may still arise. 'I want to see a solicitor about a will' may not necessarily mean that the client wishes to make a will. It is therefore sensible to **ask the client to confirm your understanding of the reason for the visit before encouraging the client to launch into a lengthy account of the facts**.

Once this confirmation has been obtained there are two matters which should be dealt with before the interview proceeds further.

(1) How is the interview to be paid for?

Clients naturally tend to be concerned about the cost of the interview and, indeed, of the job itself. Until the complete picture has been obtained, it is usually difficult to say anything meaningful about the latter and this must therefore be postponed until the closing stages of the interview.

However, as far as the cost of the interview itself is concerned, now is a good time to ascertain whether the matter and the client are covered by Community Legal Service funding. It is also essential to check if the client has the benefit of any legal expenses insurance before the interview progresses any further.

Alternatively, explain to the client what your charging rate is or, if such be the case, that the firm's policy is to charge a fixed fee, for example for an initial half-hour interview. If the firm's policy is to provide the initial interview free of charge, then it will be reassuring for the client if this is confirmed by the solicitor early on in the interview. Once the initial costs have been explained clearly to the client, you should check whether the client is genuinely content to accept this arrangement. You may like to mention that you will return to the matter of costs at the end of the interview when you have a better idea of the client's situation.

(2) How will the interview be conducted?

It makes sense to start by letting the client know how long you have available for the interview and to find out whether the client is under any time constraints.

It is also helpful to say a little about how you propose to conduct the interview:

> 'In a minute I'll ask you to explain why you have come to see me. Then I will need to ask you some questions and make some notes. Finally, when I have got the complete picture, I shall explain what your legal position is and what options I think are open to you. Between us, we can then try to decide which course of action would best suit your needs.'

When the client is a new client, this point in the interview may be a good opportunity to reassure him/her that everything he/she tells you will be held in confidence.

Skills summary

(1) Listening.
(2) Open questions.
(3) No (or very brief) note-taking.

10.5.5 Obtaining the facts

The objective is to obtain the client's account of the facts or of the proposed transaction.

This objective should be achieved by encouraging the client to give an account of the matter in his or her own words with as little interruption from you as possible.

Consider the impact on the client of the following choice of words and expressions:

'So, where shall we start?' (Doesn't inspire confidence)

'What's the problem, then?' (There may not be a 'problem')

'Thank you for sending me the documentation … It seems to me …' (Over directional – premature diagnosis)

'Things don't look too good, do they?' (Prematurely pessimistic – provokes anxiety)

'Don't worry, we'll sort this out for you.' (Prematurely optimistic – raises expectations)

'Funny, this is the sixth one we've had in like this in the last month.' (Treating client as a 'case' to be processed – not a human being)

'This is the one, I think. Now then, where are we? … Let me see … dah dah dah dah … Oh yes that's right, this is a GBH case, isn't it?' (Disorganised – unprepared – confusing use of jargon)

Clearly, therefore, you must give very careful thought to the form of words which you use to invite the client to begin this process.

If you are interviewing a client about a road accident it may be perfectly sensible to say 'Perhaps you could start by telling me exactly what happened on the day in question'.

On the other hand, if the client wishes to make a will, saying 'Could you now give me some general background information?' or 'Just tell me the story in your own words' is too vague to indicate what sort of information you require. A more focused wording would be 'It's a good idea to make a will, is there any particular reason that has prompted you to do so now?' or 'Perhaps you could start by giving me a brief summary of everything which you own and a general idea of who you are thinking of leaving it to'.

Whatever form of opening words you decide upon, it can also be helpful if, during this part of the interview, you also ask questions along the lines of 'It would also be helpful if you could let me know any particular concerns which you have,' and 'Do you foresee any problems?'

You should concentrate on using the various listening techniques discussed in **10.4.1** and confine questions to open questions which will encourage the client to continue the narrative.

There will be ample opportunity in the next stage of the interview ('Filling in the detail') to clarify matters. You should therefore resist any temptation to do so at this stage, because a series of closed questions can easily destroy the client's concentration.

For the same reason, making written notes should, if possible, be restricted to what can be written without interrupting the client's narrative flow (see **10.4.5**).

This comparatively passive role can be a difficult one to master if you are a naturally talkative person. It does, however, enable you to maintain eye contact with the client and to observe the client's general demeanour and manner of delivery. This is very helpful in building rapport with the client and in picking up body language signals about the client's feelings.

Skills summary

(1) Listening.
(2) Open questions.
(3) Brief note-taking.

10.5.6 Filling in the detail

The objective is to ensure that you obtain a full and accurate understanding and record of the relevant facts and of the client's wishes and objectives.

You will not usually be able to give the client effective advice immediately after the client has completed his or her account of the matter in the 'Obtaining the facts' stage.

In most cases, it will be necessary to ask the client to fill gaps or explain discrepancies in the narrative or to supply information which the client had not considered to be relevant.

You will also need to take written notes and check that you have correctly understood what the client has said. It may also be necessary to examine documents.

This is the stage of the interview during which you assume a more active and directive role.

Questioning skills become more important although, even at this stage, it is generally best to use the T-funnel approach (discussed in **10.4.2**). In other words, see what information can be elicited in response to open questions before pinning down the client with more specific closed questions.

It may be necessary to use some of the clarifying and probing techniques (see **10.4.2(4)**) to jog the client's memory or to explore discrepancies or weaknesses in the client's version of events.

Before completing this stage of the interview and moving on to give advice, it is important to summarise what the client has said in order to double check that you have correctly understood the position (see **10.4.2(5)**).

Skills summary

(1) Questioning – the T-funnel approach.
(2) Note-taking.
(3) Clarifying and probing.
(4) Examining documents.
(5) Summarising.

10.5.7 Advising

The solicitor:

(1) explains the legal position of the client;
(2) discusses with the client the main options (both legal and non-legal);
(3) helps the client to reach a decision/give instructions;
(4) agrees a plan of action.

Explaining the client's legal position

The client's legal position should be explained in simple and comprehensible language. You should therefore avoid jargon. Furthermore, you should be aware that the amount of information which a client can absorb is limited (see **10.4.4**).

This is the first interview. Therefore, if:

(1) the matter is not routine; or
(2) you do not have experience in the particular area of law; or
(3) the client does not insist on preliminary 'off the cuff' advice; or
(4) the matter is not urgent,

it is quite proper to postpone advising until you have had an opportunity to carry out research. It is essential to observe the rules governing solicitors who are conducting financial services work and to avoid such work unless properly authorised to conduct it.

Clients do not always need or expect to be given immediate advice.

Discussing the main options

The client is generally less interested in being given a detailed resumé of the law than in being told what courses of action are available. You should therefore identify all possible options and discuss the relative merits of each option thoroughly with the client. This will usually involve discussing the financial cost, benefits and risks of each option. It should also take account of such non-legal factors as, for example, the emotional stress of continuing litigation and any commercial considerations.

You should try to involve the client in the discussion so that you can jointly weigh the advantages and disadvantages of each option.

Helping the client to reach a decision

All major decisions concerning the case or transaction are for the client to make. It is the client's case, not the solicitor's. However, opinion is divided on how far the solicitor may recommend a course of action for the client.

There are two schools of thought.

(1) The non-directive school suggests that a solicitor should only present the options and leave it entirely to the client to decide which to follow. The advice is characterised by the preamble, 'On the one hand X, but on the other hand Y. However, it is for you to decide'.

This approach may avoid a charge of negligence if the route followed by the client proves to be the wrong option. However, it is not particularly helpful to the client. Given the status, experience and cost of solicitors, clients often expect a recommendation.

(2) The directive school involves the solicitor in taking greater control of the decision-making process.

A combination of each approach is appropriate in most cases. It is important to explain the realistic options to the client and to explore the positive and negative consequences of each. Provided the client actively participates in this explorative discussion and you actively seek the client's views and preferences, the decision will often be clear.

Furthermore, if the matter is non-urgent, difficult or complex, the client may need time to reach a considered decision.

Agreeing a future plan of action

Once key decisions have been taken, it will usually be necessary to agree a more detailed plan of campaign, ie to decide what is the best way of carrying out the course of action which has been agreed.

For example, if your client has decided to try to settle a matter by agreement rather than go to court, you will still need to decide:

- whether to approach the other side immediately or await their next move;
- whether any first approach should be made by you or the client, and if so:

    (i) whether it should be by letter, telephone or in person;
    (ii) what (if any) opening offer should be made and how far the client is prepared to go in order to settle.

As before, you should clearly explain the range of options and try to engage the client as fully as possible in the decision-making process.

Skills summary

(1) Summarising.
(2) Explaining.
(3) Listening.
(4) Note-taking.

10.5.8 Closing

Once the issues have been discussed with the client and the client has decided what needs to be done or has decided to go away and consider his/her options more carefully, there are still a number of matters to deal with before you conclude the interview.

You should always make sure that the client has had an opportunity to discuss all matters and concerns and that The Law Society's recommendations on client care have been followed.

As far as the former is concerned, make a specific point of asking the client 'Is there anything else that you want to talk about before we finish and is there anything which we've discussed which you would like me to clarify?'. This should not be treated as a meaningless ritual, and the client should be made to feel free to respond affirmatively.

Other matters of client care are contained in Rule 15 of the Solicitors' Practice Rules 1990, which is amplified in the Solicitors' Costs Information and Client Care Code

1999, both of which are set out in the Appendix to Part II of the LPC Resource Book *Pervasive and Core Topics* (Jordans). In the LPC Resource Book *Pervasive and Core Topics* (Jordans) at **10.7.1**, the following commentary is set out:

> 'At a first interview, The Law Society recommends that a client should be informed of:
>
> (1)   the name and status of the person who will be handling the case and the name of another person in the firm whom the client may contact (particularly if a problem arises);
>
> (2)   what action the solicitor will be taking on the client's behalf, including the next immediate step in the case or transaction;
>
> (3)   what action (if any) the client has to take;
>
> (4)   the likely duration of the matter, including the approximate time when the solicitor will next contact the client;
>
> (5)   the likely cost of the matter and how this cost will be funded, whether privately, by legal aid or by legal expenses insurance.'

Dealing with the points in the above order:

(1)   Name and status of person handling the case

Giving the name and status of the person who will be handling the case is something which will probably have been explained as part of the greeting or preliminaries stage of the interview. Giving the name of another person in the firm as an alternative point of contact can appropriately be dealt with as part of the closing stage of the interview. Details of any complaints procedure is something which could also be dealt with at this stage, but in practice is more commonly included in a follow-up letter written to the client after the interview.

(2)   Follow-up tasks by solicitor

During the interview, it is important to establish exactly what, if anything, the client is instructing you to do. In the closing stages of the interview, it is clearly helpful to summarise what steps you have agreed to take and when you will take them. The steps will vary from case to case but might involve taking a statement from a witness, obtaining a police or medical report, writing a letter before action, doing a company search, preparing a draft will or partnership agreement or drafting a divorce petition.

In most cases, it will be appropriate to write a follow-up letter to the client summarising what has been discussed and agreed. Telling the client that you intend to do this is obviously reassuring.

If you have not already done so, now is a good time to check that you have an accurate note of the client's address and telephone number. Check also to which address the client wishes correspondence to be sent.

(3)   Follow-up tasks by client

You should also remind the client of any action which he/she agreed to take. This might include supplying information or documents which were not available during the interview or thinking about the advice or discussing his/her options with others and contacting you once a decision has been reached.

(4) Time frame for the matter

The client should be given some indication of how long the matter will take to complete. Sometimes an estimate is quite easy to give:

> 'As the agreed terms are quite straightforward, I shall be able to send you and Simon a draft of the partnership agreement by the end of the week. Then, if you're both happy with it, it should be possible to sign the final document sometime during next week.'

In other cases, particularly where court proceedings are a possibility, it may be impossible to do more than give a very broad estimate because future developments will to a large extent be unpredictable and outside your control. Even in these situations, you should try to give some indication of time frame, even if it is only to indicate that the matter could potentially take years rather than months.

(5) Next contact

Make it clear which of you is to make the next contact. Does your client expect to hear from you or vice versa?

At the same time, tell your client whether you think that another face-to-face meeting will be necessary and (if so) why.

For example:

> 'So we've agreed that I shall do nothing until you let me know how much you want to offer to Mr Jones. I shall then write to his solicitors offering that sum in full and final settlement.

> Obviously, if they confirm in writing that he accepts, that will broadly be an end of the matter.

> On the other hand, if he rejects the offer and continues with the court action, you and I will need to meet again to give more detailed consideration to the strength of the evidence in support of your defence.'

(6) Costs estimate of matter/method of charging

As stated in **10.5.4**, it will usually be possible to explain early in the interview how the interview itself is to be paid for, but seldom possible at that stage to discuss the likely cost of the matter itself. This, together with details of possible disbursements, will therefore usually be tackled as part of the closing stage of the interview, and care should be taken not to overlook it. The matters to be covered in the information to be given to the client are laid down in the Solicitors' Costs Information and Client Care Code (1999).

Broadly speaking, you must inform the client of:

(1)   the likely overall costs;
(2)   the basis of the firm's charges;
(3)   whether the likely outcome will justify the expense.

For a more detailed study, see the LPC Resource Book *Pervasive and Core Topics* (Jordans) Part II, Professional Conduct.

Costs should be discussed in a business-like way.

You are providing a service to the client and should not therefore appear to be embarrassed at having to discuss money.

In many cases, particularly litigation, it will be necessary to make it clear to the client that only a rough estimate of the total cost can be given because of the uncertainty concerning the amount of work which may prove necessary and the time it will take. For example, 'If this matter can't be settled out of court and has to go to a full trial, the costs are likely to be well in excess of £10,000. At this stage, it's impossible to give you a precise estimate but I will report to you regularly about costs as the matter progresses'.

Skills summary

(1) Summarising (perhaps in writing).
(2) Explaining.

10.5.9 Parting

When the interview is over, you should accompany the client back to the reception area.

The parting should be friendly, courteous and (if possible) reassuring.

10.6 FURTHER READING

Students wishing to undertake further reading on the matters covered in this chapter will find any of the following books helpful.

Sherr *Client Care for Lawyers* 2nd edn (Sweet & Maxwell, 1999)
Twist *Effective Interviewing* (Blackstone Press, 1992)
Binder and Price *Legal Interviewing and Counselling* (West Publishing Co, USA, 1977).

Chapter 11

NEGOTIATION

11.1 INTRODUCTION

Lawyers spend much of their time negotiating. They have to be able to negotiate effectively in an enormous variety of circumstances. Negotiation is generally either:

(1) transaction-based (eg settling the terms of a company take-over or partnership agreement, agreeing a mutually acceptable time and date for the completion of simultaneous conveyancing transactions); or

(2) dispute resolution, where a problem has already arisen between the parties giving, for example, breach of contract, negligence, undue influence on the making of a will, unfair dismissal, ancillary relief on divorce, breach of intellectual property rights.

Both types of negotiation rely on the same principles and skills, although the application of those principles may vary according to the context. Negotiation is a complex skill but one which can be developed and refined through practice and observation.

11.2 AIMS OF NEGOTIATION

Negotiation has been defined as 'a process of interaction by which two or more parties who consider they need to be jointly involved in an outcome, but who initially have different objectives, seek by the use of argument and persuasion to resolve their differences in order to achieve a mutually acceptable solution' (Alan Fowler *Negotiation: Skills and Strategies* (IPM, 1990)).

This definition implies something different from the common perception of negotiating as a battle of wills, where necessarily one side wins at the expense of the other. Skilled negotiators are aware of the merits of achieving solutions that are seen by both sides as fair. They also realise that, by sharing as much information as possible with the other side, opportunities can arise to 'expand the cake' available to the parties. Such an approach does not mean that you accept a settlement which is against your client's best interests, but it does mean that you adopt a flexible approach; you should be open to ideas put forward by the other side and be prepared to adapt your position if new information comes to light in the negotiation.

Aspects of negotiating which this chapter seeks to encourage are:

- thorough preparation and the adoption of a logical approach when preparing;
- the use of objective standards of reference when these are available (eg audited accounts, experts' reports);
- flexible use of different negotiating styles and the avoidance of an aggressive style when this is impeding progress;
- searching for different (perhaps unconventional) solutions to problems;
- the promotion of trust between the parties;

- the production of settlements that will endure because they are perceived as fair by both (all) sides;
- the observance of high ethical standards.

11.3 THE ETHICAL ASPECTS OF NEGOTIATING

A solicitor must always act ethically in accordance with the solicitors' rules of professional conduct. A solicitor must never lie, for example by giving false information. However, there is no duty to volunteer information which is adverse to a client's position. If asked a direct question on such a point, the solicitor cannot lie, but he can refuse to answer, or offer no comment, or attempt to deflect the question (eg by offering a partial answer or by parrying with a counter-question). The other negotiator might then, of course, read between the lines of the reply and guess what the true position may be.

11.4 NEGOTIATING STYLES

11.4.1 Categories

Some writers group negotiators into two general styles with names like: hard/soft or aggressive/co-operative.

However, such categorisation can be a misleading division of a myriad of different styles. Figure 1 demonstrates this by charting two characteristics of the negotiator which are not necessarily mutually exclusive but which can be integrated with each other in widely varying degrees.

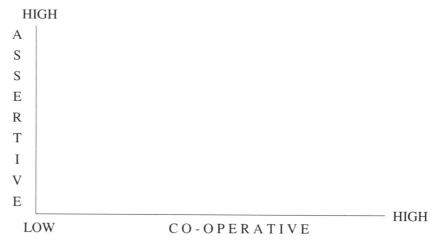

Figure 1

How assertive are you? Mark your point on the vertical axis. How co-operative are you? Mark your point on the horizontal axis. Mark on the graph where your two points meet.

This analysis recognises that everybody's style is different: there are hundreds of points on the graph. However, although it gives a general indication of a person's predominant style, the analysis still has inherent drawbacks. First, self-analysis is not always accurate. Secondly, it fails to recognise that you can and should vary your style according to the situation. Effective negotiators are highly flexible and will vary their style according to the merits of the case they are pursuing and the style adopted by the other negotiator.

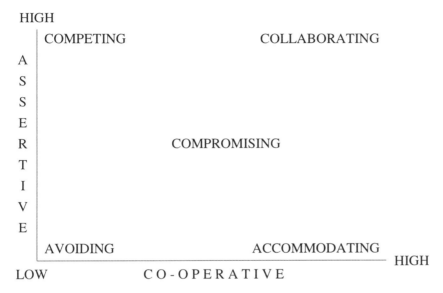

Figure 2

Figure 2 shows the same chart divided into five broad styles, any one of which can be used according to the circumstances.

It is important to:

- know the potential strengths and weaknesses of your own predominant style;
- learn to vary your own style; and
- be able to identify, and react appropriately, to the style of the other negotiator.

11.4.2 Avoiding

The avoiding style is low both on assertiveness and co-operativeness. It is sometimes used by those who are facing actual or potential legal action, or a proposed term in a transaction, against which they have little or no argument. They hope that if they ignore the problem, either it will go away or circumstances will change in their favour.

It is also an approach that might be adopted by the solicitor on one side if he knows the other side has a deadline to meet. He will be trying to put off the real negotiations until the other side is under severe time pressure, knowing that this will then put him into a strong position.

The appropriate response to an opponent who adopts an avoiding style is to press ahead as quickly as possible, perhaps by imposing time-limits or by pursuing alternative courses of action which force him into serious talks, for example by issuing and serving proceedings.

11.4.3 Accommodating

A person adopting an accommodating style is keen to accept the other side's proposals and reach agreement.

It is sometimes a style which results from the negotiator's personality. It may be consciously adopted, however, if the other side has grossly misjudged the parties' positions. Even in these circumstances, it might, in some cases, be wiser not to take advantage of the other side's error particularly when the parties will have an ongoing relationship.

11.4.4 Compromising

It is vital that negotiators should have the capacity to compromise; otherwise, deals would never be made and disputes would never be settled. A party may be prepared to compromise in order to avoid:

- the uncertainties of trial (on liability or quantum, e.g. when a witness fails to come 'up to proof');
- the possible publicity arising out of litigation;
- the delay involved in going to trial;
- the emotional stress that continued litigation could involve;
- the legal costs of going any further – even if you win in court, you are unlikely to recover all the legal costs from the unsuccessful defendant;
- the further loss of management time for a commercial client;
- the transaction falling through; or
- souring an ongoing relationship between two commercial parties or between members of a family.

The question is how and when to compromise. A compromising style might be characterised by a readiness always to 'split the difference' between the two sides' positions, regardless of the objective merits. There may sometimes be good reasons for closing the deal in this way, but they do not include the easy disposal of the matter or the speedier payment of your fees.

11.4.5 Competing

Competitors are unco-operative and highly assertive. They may or may not also be aggressive.

If you have a strong case and the other side is accommodating, a competing style can be highly effective.

On the other hand, if it is misused, the style can create mistrust, distorted communication, tension and the souring of long-term relationships. It can provoke retaliation (the other side becomes aggressive) or obstinacy (the other side digs in his heels). In either case, settlement can be severely delayed or a proposed deal can fall apart. Clients will not be grateful.

If you are faced with competitive negotiators, try to avoid counter-productive reactions. Ignore the personality and concentrate on the objective merits of the arguments. It may be helpful to ask yourself: 'Why are they behaving like this?' There could be a number of possible reasons, each of which should generate a different response from you.

(1) The behaviour might be part of their personality, their normal style. Have you or any of your colleagues negotiated with them before? Consult as widely as possible.

(2) It may be that they do in fact have a very strong case.

(3) They may have a very weak case and are therefore bluffing or over-compensating. Stay calm. Take care not to react too hastily. Bide your time until you are more certain of the objective merits of the case.

(4) They may be under-prepared. As a result, they may be worried that they are running the risk of making an error of judgement and conceding too much. They therefore over-compensate and become less co-operative and more assertive (or avoiding) in order to reduce that risk. If you suspect this to be the reason, the best tactic might be to adjourn the negotiation until they are better prepared.

(5) They may have become competitive in response to what they perceive to be your competitiveness. After a heated and unproductive negotiation, one negotiator said to a neutral observer: 'I started off in a spirit of co-operation and compromise; I was prepared to adopt a collaborative search for a mutually acceptable solution; but he was so competitive that we both ended up just going hammer and tongs at each other'. The other negotiator said exactly the same.

Ultimately, it should be remembered that in a negotiation there are no rules or procedures which have to be followed (unless you have agreed to them) and there is no obligation to reach a settlement. The other side cannot force you into anything without your consent.

11.4.6 Collaborating

Some people call collaboration 'problem-solving' or 'principled negotiation'. In theory, it is often the ideal negotiating style because it gives you the best of both worlds. Assertiveness and co-operativeness are not mutually exclusive. You can be high in both.

Assertiveness is not the same as aggression. You should aim to be sufficiently assertive to press your own client's case and to avoid being trampled on by an aggressive opponent; at the same time, you should be sufficiently co-operative to search for any possibility of a mutually beneficial solution. This is particularly important where there will be (or the parties would like there to be) a continuing business or personal relationship after the present dispute has been resolved.

Beware, however, of certain risks.

(1) Beware of wolves in sheep's clothing, ie, the pleasant negotiator who smiles a lot, flatters you, appears to be perfectly reasonable (and may pepper his statements with phrases like 'fair and reasonable' and 'sympathetic to your client's case'), but who on objective analysis is being competitive and offering very little. The moral is: do not jump to conclusions; try not to allow personality to influence you; concentrate on the objective merits of the case.

(2) If you are trying to adjust your own predominant style, for example become more assertive or become more co-operative, there is a danger that, as one characteristic increases, so the other decreases. Although it is possible to be high on both, it can be difficult to achieve.

11.4.7 Conclusion

Everyone has elements of all five styles within them. You should try to be flexible, to exploit your strengths, to minimise your weaknesses, and not to be distracted by personalities. Do not allow your own ego to intrude. Try to think about the case objectively from your client's point of view.

The rest of this chapter generally assumes a collaborative style. However, thorough preparation, self-confidence and perceptiveness are more important than personal style.

11.5 PREPARATION FOR A NEGOTIATION

11.5.1 Importance of preparation

The successful negotiator possesses many skills; these include the ability to communicate, listen, persuade, analyse and create. These talents must, however, be supported by a bedrock of knowledge.

A thorough knowledge of the facts, the law and the procedure relevant to a particular case is vital. Without that knowledge, you lose any chance of controlling the negotiating process.

It is also essential to establish clearly your client's objectives in entering into the negotiation. What is the minimum he is prepared to accept? Has he reached this position with the benefit of all available information? If he is proceeding under certain misconceptions, it is part of your role to correct them.

Armed with the requisite knowledge (law, facts and procedure) and your client's instructions, a plan based on the following sections (**11.5.2–11.5.7**) should be prepared.

11.5.2 Interests not positions

Invariably, the client will inform you of his negotiating position; he wants compensation, a fixed-term contract, the removal of a tenant. You must look behind his stated position and try to identify his underlying interests. Why does the client want what he is demanding? Ask – otherwise you may end up negotiating on the basis of false assumptions.

What are the other side's interests in entering into the negotiation? Some consideration of what these might be can help you to avoid being taken by surprise in the talks.

In addition, once the underlying interests or unspoken assumptions are identified, it may be that the underlying interests can be satisfied in some other way and at less cost than you initially expected.

Example
In negotiating a lease of the major unit in a new shopping mall, the landlord might demand from his major 'anchor' tenant absolute bars on assignment, sub-letting or change of use. The tenant might demand absolute freedom on all three. This presents an apparent impasse. However, the landlord's underlying interest might be to use the anchor tenant to attract 'satellite' tenants to the other, smaller units, while the tenant's interest might be the long-term freedom to move elsewhere. A compromise which might satisfy both parties' underlying

interests would be to have a short-term restriction rather than one which lasts for the whole duration of the lease.

Looking for underlying interests is particularly important in transaction-based negotiations or multi-issue claims. It is less likely to be productive in debt collection, personal injury or other single issue, 'money only' claims. However, it should always be investigated. For example, in debt collection it may be that the creditor has an underlying interest in the survival of the debtor's business.

11.5.3 Strengths and weaknesses

The logical next step after a consideration of the parties' underlying interests is to assess the factors which support and those which undermine your client's case (ie, once you know what he wants, what are the chances of him getting what he wants?).

Identify your client's strengths and weaknesses and those of the other side. Perhaps your client has no pressing need to make a deal but the other side has financial difficulties which make it vital for him to reach an agreement; perhaps your client's case is supported by strong legal precedent.

Once the other side's strengths have been identified, you can plan how to counter them. For example, can you obtain other evidence or reinterpret existing evidence?

What are the weaknesses in the other side's position? For example, will he risk court action if his main concern is to avoid bad publicity?

Expect the other side to have spotted the weaknesses in your client's case and to ask questions that could expose those weaknesses. Anticipate these questions and prepare carefully worded replies which (without lying or misrepresenting the position), as far as possible, protect your client.

You must, of course, behave ethically. Any misrepresentation would constitute professional misconduct, as well as rendering voidable any resulting agreement.

What questions could you ask to exploit your client's strengths and which probe for weaknesses in the other side's position? The phrasing of such questions should be carefully considered to make it difficult for the other side to avoid giving a straight (and hopefully revealing) answer. Consider whether you should use 'open' or 'closed' questioning techniques or a combination of both depending on the information you require.

To negotiate effectively you must be assertive in advancing your client's case and tenacious in seeking replies to your questions. However, this should be done within the constraints of a professional and detached approach. If the general tone of your questioning (or answers) is aggressive, sarcastic or discourteous, it is likely to sour relationships and prevent you from having productive discussions.

11.5.4 BATNA

One of the best-known books on negotiation is Fisher and Ury's *Getting to Yes*. Their acronym, BATNA, stands for Best Alternative To a Negotiated Agreement. In other words, *if the negotiations were to break down and you fail to settle*, what would you be left with? What would be the true cost or value of that alternative?

In transaction cases, your BATNA could be to do a deal with a third party rather than with the other side, or not to do a deal at all. In dispute resolution cases, the BATNA would often be litigation. Exploring the available alternatives in advance can concentrate the mind wonderfully – both your own mind and your client's. Make sure that the perceived BATNA is a realistic alternative and not just a vague possibility.

Fisher and Ury recommend that you identify, evaluate and develop your own BATNA and also try to guess the other side's. Developing your own BATNA might involve, for example, pressing ahead with litigation procedures simultaneously with trying to negotiate an out-of-court settlement.

The aim of the BATNA approach to planning a negotiation is to provide you with a yardstick against which you can assess the value of any offer made in the negotiation. Identifying your BATNA helps you to decide your 'resistance point' in the negotiation (see **11.5.5**). It can therefore protect you from being too generous, ie agreeing to give the other side more than the value of your BATNA. It can also protect you from being too obstinate, ie rejecting a final offer which is in fact better than your BATNA.

If your client appears to have an attractive alternative available, this strengthens his negotiating position; it might, therefore, be a good tactic to make the other side aware of this alternative.

In some instances, the client may have more than one alternative course of action available. If so, you should discuss with your client the feasibility of each alternative and consider whether it is worthwhile trying to develop each alternative or to concentrate on just one.

11.5.5 Issues, priorities and variables

(1) Isolation of separate issues

Many negotiations involve the resolution of several issues. It is a good idea in such cases to isolate each issue. One reason for doing this is that it helps to ensure that all relevant matters are covered in the negotiation.

> *Example*
> Your client is a retailer who has a contract with a manufacturer for the supply of an exclusive range of golfing accessories. The client has suffered losses owing to the manufacturer failing to meet agreed supply dates. He wants compensation but is aware that the stocking of the contract goods generates a great deal of his custom.
>
> The issues are:
>
> * the claim for compensation;
> * the continuation of a profitable relationship.

(2) Relative importance of each issue

Having identified the issues you should discuss with your client the relative importance to him of each to ensure you have a clear view of his priorities. In the above example, your client would almost certainly decide that the claim for compensation should not be pressed too hard if it would put at risk the continuation of the relationship.

(3) Opening bids and resistance points

On each issue, make an assessment of the most favourable result that you would hope to achieve and the least favourable result that you are prepared to accept.

MOST FAVOURABLE RESULT ('OPENING BID')

To begin by making demands which are wildly optimistic and which bear no relation to the parties' positions will result in you losing credibility. You are bound to look foolish when you are unable to give sound reasons to justify your position.

The bid you make should be the highest justifiable bid, after taking into account the law and facts which support your client's case; ie, try to predict the settlement you would obtain if all the factors which support your case were accepted, without any counter-arguments being put forward by the other side.

> *Example*
>
> Through no fault of his own, your client has been dismissed by his employer, with 2 years of a fixed-term contract left to run. His salary (after tax and national insurance deductions) was £35,000 per annum. The most favourable result would be to obtain the total of lost net salary (£70,000) for the remaining 2-year period. It is a bid which can be justified on a contractual basis.
>
> You would expect your opponent to put forward arguments which support the reduction of this figure (eg the former employee has a duty to mitigate his loss by looking for other work), but if your opponent fails to do so you could achieve a very good settlement for your client (although, bear in mind that other factors may lead you to decide not to take advantage of the other side's mistakes).

This is one of the possible benefits of aiming high at the start. Another is that if valid counter-arguments are raised, it allows you to 'come down' and offer concessions. This can be an important way of showing the other side that you have listened to and understood their case and that you are prepared to compromise. Any compromise requires 'give and take'. It allows people to save face; honour is satisfied. If, however, you refuse to move from your opening figure, the other side may perceive you as obstinate and unreasonable, and therefore might refuse to settle even when your opening figure is in fact realistic.

Generally, you should only open at your final figure if:

- it is the tradition or culture in that particular field of law; or
- you have a case or bargaining position that is obviously strong.

In either case, you should explain clearly to the other side that it really is a case of take it or leave it.

LEAST FAVOURABLE RESULT THAT, ON CURRENT INFORMATION, YOU WOULD ACCEPT ('RESISTANCE POINT')

The above process can also allow you to decide on the poorest deal your client should accept, ie, what settlement you would expect to negotiate if the other side puts forward all the relevant counter-arguments to your client's case.

The resistance point is not a 'bottom line'; it should not be rigidly adhered to if further information which affects your client's position comes to light in the negotiation. You must be flexible enough to take on board the significance of any new information and adapt your expectations accordingly.

Deciding on the resistance point is complicated by two other factors. First, in cases where your client has an acceptable alternative course of action, the resistance point is the point below which the client is likely to receive less from the negotiation than could be obtained by pursuing the BATNA. For example, you might decide that (even after taking into account the extra costs) your client would receive more than is currently being offered by allowing the court to decide on the level of compensation.

Secondly, your client may have given you instructions not to settle below a certain figure. If you think he is being unrealistic you should try to persuade him to adopt a more sensible position, but if he will not be moved you must comply with his instructions.

With multi-issue negotiations, the position becomes even more complicated. You might be prepared to go below your resistance point on one issue if it means you would obtain a favourable result on another. It is important to keep the whole package in mind.

Your client's priorities are the key to the decisions you make in this area. Items which are of no great significance to your client could be conceded altogether in exchange for concessions which are of more importance to him.

(4) Variables and unorthodox approaches

Another consideration in assessing the opening bid and resistance point will be the existence of 'variables'. Variables are those factors which allow for some give and take in the negotiation and which could therefore help to achieve a settlement. For example, your client might be prepared to pay a higher amount of compensation if she is allowed to pay by instalments rather than in one lump sum.

Other examples of variables which can be brought into play (depending on the subject matter of the negotiation) are inclusion/exclusion of costs, payment in a different currency, promises of future orders, quantity of goods (eg buy more, but at a lower price per unit), quality of goods (eg buy a lower grade at a lower price).

Sometimes, there may be other (perhaps unconventional) ways to resolve problems which have benefits for both sides. In Fisher and Ury's terms, you should try to 'invent options for mutual gain'.

> *Example*
> You are acting for a business which runs a parcel delivery service. One of its business customers is threatening to take action against your client because of its failure to deliver a consignment of goods. The goods have disappeared and the customer is asking for compensation. An orthodox settlement would involve a cash payment to the customer. A different approach would be to offer to make free deliveries for that customer over an agreed period. Such an offer could represent a good deal for the customer but could still be a cheaper solution for your client compared to a cash payment (the deliveries could probably be accommodated within its regular delivery service and so would not add greatly to overall costs). This approach also gives your client a chance to rebuild the customer's confidence in its service, making it less likely that the customer will go elsewhere in the future.

11.5.6 Prediction of the result (settlement zones)

Can you identify a possible settlement zone? The planning in **11.5.1–11.5.5** all leads to this. You can only decide on your final strategy if you have already worked through those stages. Your final strategy must use them and be consistent with them.

Identifying a possible settlement zone involves:

(1) deciding on:

    – your client's opening bid; and

    – his current resistance point (ie, the process described in **11.5.5**. Avoid the creation of false expectations on your client's part by ensuring that he appreciates the difference between a resistance point and a bottom line);

(2) making an educated guess at the other side's opening bid and resistance point;

(3) in the negotiation, constantly re-assessing (1) and (2) in the light of new information.

The settlement zone, if it exists at all, lies between the resistance points of the two sides. All negotiators go through the above process, more or less consciously, but it is helpful to do so methodically.

Example

In the above example of the dismissed employee, it was established that his opening bid should be in the region of £70,000. Assume that his solicitor has advised him that the least favourable result he would expect is a payment of £20,000 (taking into account the duty to mitigate the loss and the current job market for the client's skills). The employer, on the other hand, has been advised that a payment of £17,500 is probably the best result it could hope to achieve but it is prepared to pay up to £35,000, if necessary, to avoid any bad publicity that the case might generate and so that management time is not wasted on preparation for a court action.

As illustrated by *Figure 3*, the settlement zone is between £20,000 and £35,000.

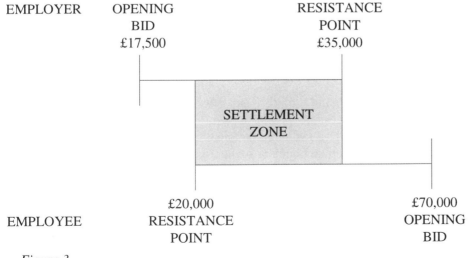

Figure 3

(4) Having identified the settlement zone, try to predict the result you would expect to achieve on all of the relevant issues, bearing in mind the respective positions of the parties.

11.5.7 Opening statement

When you have reached a decision on your negotiating strategy, you are then in a position to decide on the content of your opening statement.

There are several points to consider (see **11.8.3**), but a basic consideration at the preparatory stage is to decide upon the information you would want to disclose to the other side at this early point in the talks.

In most cases, the more information you communicate to the other side the better the chance of reaching an agreement. In particular, there are usually interests which are common to both sides; these should be stressed at the start.

The sharing of information develops trust between the parties and helps to create the climate for successful talks.

There will, however, be some information that you correctly decide not to reveal, either because it is damaging to your client's position (in which case you would hope to avoid disclosing it at any stage) or because you would prefer to introduce it later for tactical reasons (eg you intend to put it forward as a concession to the other side at the bargaining stage).

11.6 THE FORUM FOR THE NEGOTIATION

The forum for negotiation could be correspondence, telephone, a meeting or any combination of the three.

At the outset, choose the most appropriate medium for your client's case, and then be prepared to change if it proves appropriate. For example, in many cases you might start by using correspondence, but that could later become unnecessarily rigid and time-consuming. It may be wise to suggest a meeting when you have developed a strong enough case to be able to take advantage of face-to-face contact.

Correspondence

Correspondence has the following features:

- it is capable of being orderly and reasoned, and is therefore especially appropriate at the outset of complex cases;
- it gives people time to think and therefore to avoid over-hasty decisions;
- there is a risk that certain points in a letter may be left unanswered in the reply;
- some solicitors find it easier to be assertive on paper;
- it contains no non-verbal signals ('body language');
- it can lead to delay – either as a tactic, or because ambiguities or omissions are not rectified immediately;
- it is more difficult to trade concessions.

Telephone

Negotiation conducted by telephone has the following features:

- it is quick and useful for resolving one point;
- make sure you are properly prepared. It is better to be the person making the call. If you are the receiver, consider saying that you will call back at an agreed time so that you have the opportunity to prepare properly;
- there is no body language, but tones of voice are more noticeable. Silences are even more powerful on the telephone than in meetings. Use silence yourself, and do not be tempted to fill silences with a remark you may regret;
- some solicitors find it more difficult to be assertive on the telephone than in correspondence; and vice versa;
- there is a risk that either of the parties could subsequently 're-interpret' what was said.

Meetings

Meetings have the following features:

- they are immediate;
- they give greater commitment to explore the case thoroughly and/or to settle;
- body language and silences are readily apparent and capable of use;
- they are more fluid and give greater possibilities of fine movements, nuances, and the trading of concessions;
- some solicitors regard the suggestion of a meeting as a sign of weakness; others regard it as a sign of strength.

Some solicitors have a fear of meetings because of the possibility of making a decision which is later regretted, or accidentally revealing a weakness, or generally feeling uncomfortable in a potentially adversarial face-to-face role. If, however, a meeting would objectively be in the client's best interests, you should try to overcome any fears by thorough preparation and practice which will increase your self-confidence.

11.7 OTHER CONSIDERATIONS BEFORE A MEETING

11.7.1 Are you ready to negotiate?

Do not be forced into premature negotiations, which will needlessly increase costs. It is usually advisable to defer talks until you are in possession of all the information you can reasonably expect to collect.

11.7.2 Venue

In some fields of law, there is a tradition that meetings will take place at the offices of the seller or claimant. What if you have a choice? What are the factors to bear in mind?

Having the meeting at your own firm's premises gives you the feeling of control. You have full access to your papers and to the office's secretarial, catering and other facilities. Also, you do not have to suffer the time, cost and general inconvenience of having to travel.

Attending a meeting at the other side's offices might therefore be a disadvantage. However, the travelling time can sometimes enable you to arrive fresher and more fully prepared. Also, enabling the other side to feel at ease in their own offices might induce them to be more collaborative.

A third possibility is to agree a neutral venue.

11.7.3 Agree the time and length of the meeting

As a matter of courtesy to the other side, you should inform them of the time you can devote to the meeting on the agreed date.

11.7.4 Attendance at the meeting

How many people from each side will be attending? Find out their names and roles in advance. If a number of people will be attending, who will chair the meeting – the host, the person who suggested the meeting, or some other person?

Will clients also be present? Often, they are present at transaction-based negotiations but not at litigation-based meetings. Sometimes clients sit in separate side-rooms or make themselves available for telephone calls or faxes in order to give instructions to their solicitors during the meeting.

It may be a good idea to have clients present at the meeting so that an agreement can be hammered out there and then, particularly if you think:

- the major problem has been a lack of communication between the respective clients; or
- your own client is being unrealistic; or
- the other solicitor is the problem (eg not settling a case which his or her client wants to settle); and
- you can trust your own client (preparation of roles is vital); and
- you trust the other solicitor not to seek to undermine your authority in front of your own client.

Conversely, you might not wish to have clients present where there are personality clashes between the different clients or where you have an intimidating client who might hamper your style.

11.7.5 Seating arrangements

Who will sit where? What ambience do you want to try to create? To sit face to face across a table from each other is more likely to appear adversarial, whereas seating placed at a 90 degree angle is likely to appear more collaborative.

11.7.6 Clarify the purpose of the meeting

Is the meeting to be exploratory only, or is there a possibility of settling? If the latter, check that those attending will have authority to settle on behalf of their respective clients.

11.7.7 The agenda

In a multi-issue case, try to agree the agenda with the other side in advance.

If possible, try to arrange the order of issues on the agenda in a way which will enable you to test their negotiating pattern and their willingness to trade concessions before reaching an item which is of critical importance to your own client.

11.7.8 Decide your strategy

Examples of matters you might like to consider are:

- your opening position;
- the amount and the sequence of the concessions you might be prepared to offer; and
- what disclosures to make and when.

However, you should be prepared to be flexible.

11.7.9 Which party should make the first bid?

In some fields of law, the issue of which person makes the first bid is determined partly by tradition. For example, in property transactions, the solicitor acting for the landlord or seller draws up the draft lease or contract. In litigation, if the claim is for a liquidated sum (eg a contractual debt), the opening bid belongs to the claimant. If the claim is for unliquidated damages, in certain cases (eg personal injury claims) there is an argument that the claimant should simply wait until the defendant makes an acceptable Part 36 offer or payment.

Where the position is not clear-cut, the advantages of going first are that it allows you to exert an immediate and powerful influence and it shows confidence. The disadvantage is that you risk misjudging the bid.

Even if you do not wish to make the first bid, you might still like to make the first opening statement, so that you can try to establish the climate of the negotiation.

11.7.10 Final preparation for the meeting

Reread the file, and refresh your mind on key documents, facts, dates and names.

Make sure that you know your client's position on the issues and on all the possible variables. If no agenda has been agreed, prepare one now.

11.8 OVERVIEW OF A NEGOTIATION

Every negotiation should have a beginning, a middle and an end. It should be an agreed, structured process (like the order of advocacy in court hearings); otherwise, there is the risk that it will degenerate into chaos, with continual sniping and cross-fire. As a general principle, the wheels of a negotiation are oiled by good structure and management. As with interviewing and advising, structure and management interrelate with personal communication skills: each promotes the other.

Structure	*A possible strategy*
Opening	Aiming high
Discussion and bargaining	Probing Searching for variables Trading concessions Keeping whole package in mind

Closing

11.9 THE OPENING

11.9.1 Creating the climate

The opening phase of a negotiation is important for two reasons. First, it creates the climate for the negotiation. Patterns, styles and pecking order establish themselves early and are difficult then to change.

Secondly, energy and concentration are high at the outset of the negotiations but later may deteriorate.

11.9.2 Ground rules

The host of the meeting should, after effecting any necessary introductions, confirm the ground rules for the meeting, for example:

- the purpose of the meeting;
- whether or not it is 'without prejudice' and/or 'subject to contract';
- the likely length of the meeting;
- the agenda; and
- who will make the first opening statement.

11.9.3 Your opening statement

Proper, well-prepared opening statements are a great help to most negotiation meetings. They:

- help to reinforce the climate established at the outset of the meeting;
- provide structure and order (an analogy can be drawn with court trials – the advocates' opening addresses set the scene; cross-examination etc comes later);
- help everyone to 'settle down';
- remind everyone of the background, the areas of agreement, and the areas of dispute;
- help to avoid unintentional false assumptions from hindering the communication process.

Unless you have sound tactical reasons for not following them, there are some general rules relating to opening statements.

Do:

- consider saying how long your statement will take, if it is likely to be more than two or three minutes;

- if your opening statement is going to contain a bid, explain your reasoning *before* disclosing the actual bid. This increases the chances of the other side listening properly to your reasons. Otherwise, they will be thinking about the figure and their response rather than your reasons;
- present your case concisely and confidently;
- use collaborative tone, posture and gestures (unless you have decided to adopt a competitive style);
- observe carefully the other side's verbal and non-verbal reactions;
- remember the one-third rule (see **9.1**).

Don't:

- express your assumptions of the other side's interests and priorities, as this could annoy or antagonise them. Allow them to make their own case in their opening statement;
- allow them to interrupt or side-track you;
- speak for too long.

11.9.4 The other side's opening statement

It is important that you:

- listen carefully – use all the passive listening techniques (see **9.2.1**);
- concentrate on identifying their underlying interests;
- evaluate their style;
- remain non-committal on their proposals and arguments – indicate under-standing, if you can, without indicating agreement;
- take brief notes (this can be a useful way of concealing your immediate reactions).

At the end of their opening statement:

- seek clarification if necessary. Do not allow pride to deter you – you must be sure you understand exactly what they are saying. Negotiations can easily break down because of simple miscommunication;
- summarise;
- stress areas of agreement;
- make sure that they have told you the whole of their 'shopping list', to reduce the risk of being ambushed later by a last-minute demand.

Do not concentrate too much on mentally drafting or rehearsing your own rebuttal, as this will hinder your listening to and understanding their case, and do not interrupt (unless you have deliberately chosen to be competitive).

11.10 THE MIDDLE PHASE: DISCUSSION AND BARGAINING

Statements generate resistance
Questions generate answers
Silence generates discomfort, answers, new suggestions.
(adapted from a passage in *Getting to Yes* by Fisher and Ury)

'I don't go in to do all the talking. Quite the opposite.
I go in to do the listening because that's the best bit.'
(Insurance company chief claims inspector, quoted in *Hard Bargaining* by Hazel Genn)

11.10.1 Discussion

During the discussion:

(1) demonstrate that you have heard and understood what the other side has said even if you do not agree with them;

(2) in the middle phase of a negotiation, you should probe the other side's case with a mixture of appropriate open and closed questions.

   You could question any of the following:

   – any assumptions you think they might be making;
   – their underlying interests or needs ('Why does your client want … ?');
   – whether or not there may be other ways of meeting those interests;
   – the criteria or evidence to justify their bid ('What criteria did you use to arrive at … ?', 'What evidence have you got to support … ?', 'Where did you get that evidence from?');
   – their interpretation of the law or of the facts; or
   – analogous or comparable circumstances or cases they have had.

   Do not ask two questions at once.

   Give them time to answer – do not be tempted to fill a silence too quickly.

   Listen and observe carefully when they answer. Was there any hesitation, uncertainty or discomfort?

   If necessary, re-phrase crucial questions so that all the angles are covered.

   Do not allow them to use diversionary tactics such as answering a question with a question, or changing the subject. Be courteous but firm;

(3) spell out the weaknesses of their position calmly and firmly;

(4) be prepared to answer their questions with a judicious mixture of firm replies, silences and counter-questions. Try to maintain a confident tone of voice and posture;

(5) review the progress of the discussions at appropriate intervals. If there is an impasse, or one aspect is taking too long, consider the following:
   – summarise – this can give you the opportunity to stress the areas on which you have already reached agreement and so reinforce the climate for agreement; it can also give you time to think and, if appropriate, to try to redirect the negotiation;
   – defer further discussion of the particular topic until later in the negotiation;

(6) explore the possibility of settling issues on the basis of objective criteria. For example, you might agree to accept the opinion of an independent expert as a way to resolve the problem. An advantage of this approach is that neither party can feel cheated by the other; another is that you are more likely to achieve a fair result, which can have particular benefits where the parties will have an ongoing relationship.

11.10.2 Bargaining

Generally, you will only have agreed to a meeting (other than a purely exploratory meeting) if both parties are prepared to compromise, ie to bargain.

Although you might bargain item by item or clause by clause in multi-issue cases, try to keep the whole package in mind. It might be sensible not to finalise an agreement on any particular issue until the shape of the whole agreement is clear (including, for example, costs).

Keep searching for variables, for example: time for payment; payment in a different currency; a promise of future orders or the grant of options; performance-related payments; performance in stages.

Bargaining involves the trading of concessions. Compromise is achieved by both parties moving from their original positions. On the assumption that the other side has aimed high, you should be cautious about accepting their first offer.

A competitive negotiator might refuse to concede anything to you for some time, and then concede only small amounts, slowly and at irregular intervals, and of diminishing amounts. Such a strategy is clearly designed to lower your expectations. However, if in fact there is a significant margin between that negotiator's opening bid and resistance point, the strategy carries the risk of a relatively sudden but very late climb-down (eg a 'door-of-the-court' settlement). If you suspect that this strategy is being used against you, consider abbreviating the negotiation and press ahead with your BATNA (Best Alternative To a Negotiated Agreement) – for example, by pressing ahead with the litigation if you are a claimant or making a Part 36 payment if you are a defendant.

When you are offered a concession, it is a question of judgement whether you express appreciation for it, or emphasise the lack of cost to them, or both.

When making a concession, emphasise the cost to you of it and try to give a reason for it. For example, you can often relate it to something the other side has said in the negotiation. Your concession can thus demonstrate that you have taken their point and responded accordingly, rather than appear to be arbitrary.

In order to avoid 'giving away' a concession with nothing in return, or in order to try to move the negotiation forward, always consider offering conditional or hypothetical concessions: 'We could move on X but only if you could move on Y'; 'I have no authority from my client on this point, but what if X?'. Although these statements might be interpreted to mean that, if pushed, you would be prepared to concede unreservedly, it is a risk that parties have to take in the dynamics of a negotiation.

Make sure you take appropriate notes and, in particular, keep a record of all concessions or agreements.

11.10.3 Adjournments

Adjournments can be very useful.

The length of an adjournment will depend on its purpose. It could be for as little as ten minutes, for example, in order to have a brief strategy review (on your own, with a colleague, or with your client), or for as long as several weeks or months in order to await the availability of further evidence.

Other reasons for suggesting an adjournment include:

- alertness waning;
- to help resolve an impasse or deadlock;

- to allow a heated atmosphere to cool down; or
- to try to 'close the deal' during the relative informality of a refreshment break.

11.10.4 Resolving deadlocks

In cases of deadlock, the following actions should be considered:

- defer an item on the agenda;
- search for variables;
- adjourn; or
- refer to an alternative dispute resolution ('ADR') process (see **11.13**).

11.11 THE END: CLOSING A NEGOTIATION

11.11.1 When?

The timing of the close of a negotiation will depend on a cost-benefit analysis. How much more do you think you can achieve? Compare the expected achievements against the cost to the client in terms of time, money and stress. Will further negotiation be cost effective? This analysis needs to be conducted at regular intervals. Beware of a variation of Parkinson's Law: 'negotiating expands to fill the time allotted to it'.

11.11.2 How?

A number of tactics can be used to signal to the other side that you see the end in sight.

- 'Last rites' – summarise the position reached, emphasising the concessions you have made and the extent and reasonableness of your movement: 'We have reached our final position';
- Use a refreshment break to suggest informally that the end is near;
- Give a deadline or ultimatum;
- Make a concession and express it as a final gesture to settle;
- If the gap between the sides is small, either suggest, or try to induce the other side to suggest, that you 'split the difference';
- If there is one outstanding point, you might be able to agree that the point be adjudicated by an agreed independent third party.

11.11.3 The agreement

Do not allow the euphoria of reaching agreement to distract you from other important and immediate tasks, such as:

- confirming what has been agreed;
- preparing an immediate agreed written summary;
- ensuring that details are clarified in order to avoid later disputes; and
- preparing a list of actions to be taken (if appropriate) by both sides.

11.12 'DIRTY TRICKS'

The phrase 'dirty tricks' is used loosely, and is not necessarily confined to misconduct. You need to be aware of such tricks, not so that you can use them, but in order to both be able to recognise them when they are used against you and, if possible, be able to counter them. They include the following.

11.12.1 Surprise attacks

Surprise attacks can take the form of sudden changes in tactics or demands, intimidation, withdrawal of offers or emotional outbursts. They are often designed to throw you off balance, undermine your confidence, and create anxiety and a desire to placate or settle quickly.

Try to remain unperturbed. Try not to retaliate. If you find it difficult to continue to focus on the merits of the case, consider questioning the other side's tactics openly or calling an adjournment.

11.12.2 'Good guy, bad guy'

The 'good guy, bad guy' tactic is sometimes used by a negotiating team of lawyers, or a solicitor who wishes to portray his client as hard and uncompromising.

The aim of the tactic is to capitalise on the relief felt at evading the 'bad guy'. Again, you should try to continue to focus on the merits of the case.

11.12.3 Feinting

Feinting is where the solicitor seems to attach great importance to one particular item. He then concedes it in order to 'soften you up' for another item in which he expresses little interest but which is, in fact, far more important to his client.

Do not take things at face value.

11.12.4 False deadlines

False deadlines can sometimes be tested by saying 'We might be able to offer more, but we will not know until after [the date of the deadline]'.

11.12.5 Limited authority/reneging on 'agreements'

Always make sure at the time of the agreement that it is explicit whether or not the solicitor has the authority to settle, whether the agreement is final, and record the position in writing. If you do not, you may think that a case has been settled only to receive a letter stating, for example: 'I reported on our provisional agreement. My client is fairly happy with it, but there is just one matter …'.

11.12.6 Last-minute demands

Make sure you obtain all the other side's demands at the outset. This will make it less likely that they will surprise you with a sudden new demand.

11.12.7 Environmental controls

If the seating arrangements or environment of the meeting room make you feel uncomfortable, you should immediately and politely ask for them to be changed.

11.12.8 Lying

Try to take accurate notes of key points without being distracted from the negotiation. If you can later prove that the other side lied during the negotiation, then the settlement could be rescinded for misrepresentation and, where a solicitor knowingly lied, the matter could be reported to The Law Society as professional misconduct.

11.13 ALTERNATIVE DISPUTE RESOLUTION

11.13.1 What is it?

Alternative dispute resolution (ADR) is not a term of art: it includes any process of dispute resolution other than litigation, arbitration or traditional negotiation between the parties or their solicitors. The commonest form of ADR is mediation.

The object of litigation, arbitration, negotiation or ADR is to provide a process which efficiently and effectively resolves a dispute. Which of the four, or which combination of them is best, will depend on the circumstances of each case.

The essential ingredients of ADR are:

(1) it is a voluntary, private process. The parties cannot be forced to use ADR; if they do use it, they can control the mechanics and rules of the process; and they can withdraw from it at any time unless and until they make a contractually binding out-of-court settlement or agreement;

(2) there is a third party neutral (often a mediator) who facilitates settlement, often by 'shuttlecock' diplomacy, but who has no power to order or impose a solution on the parties.

In essence, ADR is intended to be an efficient and structured form of negotiation involving a third party. It can thus be interposed between traditional negotiating and litigation (or arbitration): if traditional negotiating fails, try an ADR process; if that fails, then either stalemate or litigation (or arbitration) remains.

Since the introduction of the Civil Procedure Rules in 1999, ADR has been actively promoted by the civil courts. The recent case of *Dunnett v Railtrack plc (in Railway Administration)* [2002] EWCA Civ 303, [2002] 2 All ER 850 highlighting the parties duty to consider seriously the possibility of ADR procedures being used to help resolve their claim. In that case, Brook LJ emphasised the potential of ADR to 'achieve results satisfactory to both parties in many cases which are quite beyond the power of lawyers and courts to achieve'. Railtrack despite succeeding in having the claimant's appeal dismissed were not awarded their costs because they had refused to contemplate ADR when approached at a stage before the costs of the appeal began to flow.

Although usually used in the litigation field, ADR can also be used in commercial transactions. First, a commercial contract could incorporate an ADR clause, ie, a non-binding (but influential) promise that if any dispute later arises between the parties, they will refer that dispute to an ADR process before resorting to litigation or arbitration.

Secondly, if parties are negotiating the terms of a transaction and reach an impasse on one particular term, they could agree to refer that one item to an ADR process.

11.13.2 The advantages

Like traditional negotiating, ADR can be quicker, cheaper and more private, and produce more flexible terms of settlement, than litigation or arbitration.

The third party neutral:

- can provide a view that is perceived by both parties as being more objective;
- by shuttlecock diplomacy may be able to identify potential solutions that neither party alone could see; and
- has a better chance of preserving relationships between the parties.

This last point can be very important in commercial or family disputes, but is less so where neither party has any intention of continuing any future relationship with the other.

11.13.3 The disadvantages

(1) One reason why ADR is relatively quick and cheap is that the evidence is not investigated or examined as thoroughly as in litigation or arbitration: instead, only what are thought to be the key issues and interests are explored. Parties cannot have it both ways, ie, a wide, in-depth investigation which is also quick and cheap. In each case, it is a question of choosing the lesser of two evils.

(2) Because ADR is a voluntary process, it is not appropriate when one party needs immediate judicial relief by way of an interlocutory injunction.

(3) Likewise, ADR is unlikely to resolve 'non-genuine' disputes, for example where a defendant is clearly stalling for time and refusing to admit liability simply in order to hang on to his money for as long as possible.

(4) ADR is not appropriate in 'test cases' where you want a binding, judicial precedent, for example the correct legal interpretation of a clause in a standard form contract.

11.14 FURTHER READING

Fisher, Ury and Patton *Getting to Yes* (Random House, 1997)
Scott *The Skills of Negotiating* (Gower Publishing, 1986)
Halpern *Negotiating Skills* (Blackstone Press, 1992)
Kennedy *Everything is Negotiable* (Arrow Books, 1997)
Williams *Legal Negotiation and Settlement* (West Publishing Co, USA, 1983)
Foskett *The Law and Practice of Compromise* (Sweet & Maxwell, 2002)
Lax and Sebenius *The Manager as Negotiator: Bargaining for Co-operation and Competitive Gain* (Prentice Hall, 1987)

Chapter 12

ADVOCACY

12.1 INTRODUCTION

In answer to the question 'Are good advocates born or made?', most people would say: 'They're born. Advocacy is not one of those things which can be taught'. Many lawyers would probably say the same. Skilled advocates are seen as being eloquent, articulate, and able to think on their feet: all qualities which at first sight seem to be innate rather than acquired. Undoubtedly, some advocates are more naturally gifted than others, but many of these so-called gifts can be acquired through hard work and practice. Perhaps the worst mistake is to assume that good advocacy is simply a matter of flair, and little else. The advocate who demolishes an opponent's witness in cross-examination rarely achieves this by jumping to his feet and firing off the first thing that comes into his head; a great deal of thought and preparation will have gone into every aspect of the challenge he makes.

This chapter gives a basic introduction to advocacy. For those who wish to practise as advocates, it represents the first stage of a continuous learning process. However, others may never appear before a court as an advocate at any stage of their professional careers. Even so, the skills covered in this chapter will prove useful in any situation where effective oral presentation is required.

12.2 SKILLS

The skills of an advocate divide into oral skills and organisation skills.

12.2.1 Oral skills

Advocates are skilled talkers: this is an obvious point which should never be overlooked. Within the stylised atmosphere of the courtroom the task of the advocate, subject to the rules of professional conduct, is to talk his way to the best result that can be obtained for his client. The three major oral skills are as follows.

Presentation
Every advocate needs to be a good storyteller, especially when he is opening a case on behalf of either the prosecution or the claimant. It is not generally realised that a court may know next to nothing about the facts of the case it is about to try or the issues involved: it therefore needs to be put in the picture in a way which will engage its interest.

Argument
Every advocate also needs to be a good persuader. Much of an advocate's time will be spent addressing the court with a view to persuading it to find in favour of his

client. Argument may be as to the overall issue of guilt or liability, or as to a subsidiary issue such as bail, the grant of an interim order, or a point of law.

Questioning witnesses

The questioning of witnesses is the skill which young advocates tend to find the most complex and difficult to master. English trials are characterised not only by their adversarial nature but also by the fact that much evidence is still given orally. The ability to extract the relevant evidence from your own witnesses by means of examination-in-chief and to challenge the testimony of an opponent's witnesses in cross-examination is still seen as the most important attribute of the experienced advocate.

In the course of a civil or criminal trial, all three of the above skills will be exercised, but in many other situations, advocacy will consist almost exclusively of presentation and argument. This is particularly true of the vast majority of chambers applications in civil cases, because evidence will almost invariably be given by witness statements. Bail applications and pleas in mitigation in criminal cases also involve very little questioning of witnesses.

12.2.2 Organisation skills

In addition to the oral skills, a good advocate also draws upon other back-up skills which are exercised outside the court room. When an experienced advocate is performing in court, it all seems effortless: he has all the facts at his fingertips, nothing seems to throw him off his stride, and witnesses are examined and cross-examined incisively and in a logical sequence. On top of this, he manages to maintain the appearance of being calm and dignified at the most crucial moments, and never loses his temper. At all times, he is courteous to the court, his opponent, and the most recalcitrant witnesses. To the uninitiated it may look easy, but this level of competence is achieved only by hard work and experience. It is also dependent upon the advocate having thoroughly prepared and organised the case beforehand.

The most important organisation skills are set out below: there is nothing magical about any of them, in fact some of them may appear positively mundane, but no advocate can do without them.

Fact gathering and analysis

No advocate can begin to prepare a case until he has thoroughly mastered its facts. Until this is done, it is impossible to analyse its strengths and weaknesses. Ignorance of the facts will also make it far more difficult to perform adequately in court. For example, when cross-examining a witness it will often be necessary to fire a sequence of rapid questions in order to try and shake his testimony. The task will be made immeasurably easier if the advocate's mastery of the facts is such that there is little or no need to refer to prepared notes before proceeding to the next question. Many readers will have seen US courtroom dramas on television in which advocates never use notes. In real life they are trained to memorise the whole case file. Although UK courtroom style is very different, advocates should try to rely on notes as little as possible.

Knowledge of the relevant law

It is essential to research the relevant substantive law. The advocate must also develop a detailed knowledge of the law of evidence and the relevant procedural law. So far as evidence is concerned, it will always be necessary to study the relevant facts carefully in order to analyse:

(1) what the issues are;
(2) which issues are in dispute;
(3) who has the burden of proof; and
(4) what admissible evidence is available to prove or disprove those issues.

However, that is not enough; you will also need to memorise as much of the law of evidence as you can since an evidential problem may arise unpredictably during the course of a trial. Advocates rarely have time to look the law up in advance of raising an objection.

Similarly, procedural points have a habit of cropping up unexpectedly: an advocate's effectiveness will be greatly enhanced if his level of knowledge is such that these can be identified as soon as they arise.

Handling paperwork

In some respects, handling paperwork is the most neglected organisation skill of all, but it is in fact one of the most important, especially in civil cases. Even quite simple cases can end up producing masses of papers, some of which may need to be referred to at some time during a case. It is important therefore not only to devise a system which enables a required document to be located at a moment's notice, but also to know the contents of every document. This is particularly vital in chambers applications in civil proceedings so far as witness statements are concerned. The master or district judge may intervene by suddenly asking a question on a particular issue. The advocate should immediately be able to refer him to the relevant paragraph in the appropriate witness statements.

The ability to handle paperwork is also important in civil trial advocacy with rules requiring pre-trial exchange of witness statements.

12.3 THE BASICS

This section contains a simple checklist to assist in preparation of a case. It also deals with wider aspects of court behaviour and protocol.

12.3.1 Preparation

Good advocacy depends on planning and preparation at every stage. In particular, the order in which you address each task needs to be carefully considered so as to achieve the maximum benefit. The following checklist should always be followed.

Master the relevant facts

If the facts are simple, try to commit them to memory. In more complicated cases, prepare a written chronology for reference purposes which should ideally then be memorised as far as possible.

Analyse the facts

By applying the appropriate substantive, evidential and procedural law you should be able to identify the following:

(1) the legal issues in dispute. Consider in this context whether there are any submissions you will need to make, for example as to admissibility;

(2) the factual issues in dispute. Identify what findings of fact the court will have to make if your client's case is to succeed;

(3) develop a 'theory' of the case consistent with your client's instructions. The more plausible the case advanced, the more likely it is to succeed.

Based upon the analysis above, plan objectives for each stage at which you will be called upon to speak or examine witnesses.

12.3.2 Presentation

Although presentation has been categorised as a specific oral skill, every aspect of the advocate's courtroom role in effect involves conducting a presentation, not only of the client's case but also of the advocate himself. The following list sets out a number of presentational rules which should always be followed.

(1) Maintain eye contact with the person whom you are addressing.

(2) Never read from a prepared text.

(3) Be aware of 'body language'. The way in which an advocate behaves can affect the court's perceptions of his case. Try always to bear the following points in mind:

    (a) Stand still. Advocates who are nervous have a tendency to sway from side to side.

    (b) Stand up straight when in open court. Make sure you know your case well enough to avoid frequent references to your papers.

    (c) Do not speak with your hands in front of your face. This is another common mannerism when a speaker is nervous. Be especially conscious of this trait in chambers proceedings where advocates remain seated.

    (d) Keep your hands and arms still (within reason). Although arm and hand gestures can sometimes be an effective means of emphasising a point they should be used sparingly.

    (e) Keep your emotions under control. To be an effective advocate you will need to be able to hide all kinds of feelings. For example, never appear shocked because a witness says the opposite to what you expect. Learn to sail on unperturbed through the most stormy waters.

(4) Speak slowly in a clear, low tone. If you are anxious, you are likely to speak quickly and in a high voice. In particular, always 'watch the judge's pen'. You are hardly likely to be persuasive if the court cannot keep up with you. The same rule applies when taking the court through documents: it takes time for them to read them and digest their contents.

(5) Do not be afraid of pauses. What may seem to the advocate to be a long gap in presentation is often not even noticed by the court.

(6) Avoid being long-winded and unnecessarily repetitive. These are both traits which suggest that you have not prepared the case very well.

(7) Know your court. All your planning must be with a view to persuading the court of the strength of your case. It is perhaps obvious but nevertheless important to

realise that, for example, a judge will need to be addressed differently from a lay magistrate. Tailor your style to suit your audience.

(8) Be honest and courteous. At all times, bear in mind the need to build and maintain your reputation with the court. The advocate who loses the court's trust is of no use to his client. Always be scrupulously courteous to the court and to your opponent, even if you are disappointed with the way your case has gone.

12.3.3 How to address the court

Nothing reveals an advocate's lack of experience more than a failure to adopt the correct mode of address. The following list should therefore be committed to memory:

Court	*Mode of address*
High Court Judge:	'My Lord' or 'My Lady' as appropriate
Circuit Judge:	'Your Honour'
Recorder:	'Your Honour'
District Judge of the High Court or County Court:	'Sir' or 'Madam' as appropriate
District Judge of the magistrates' court:	'Sir' or 'Madam' as appropriate
Master of the Supreme Court:	'Master'
Supreme Court Costs Judge:	'Master'
Magistrates (lay and stipendiary):	'Sir' or 'Madam' as appropriate.

In the magistrates' court, 'Your worships' is technically incorrect, but frequently used and indeed preferred by many lay benches.

A particular problem is whether it is appropriate to address the court in the second person singular ('You'). In the case of district judges, masters and magistrates, it is perfectly permissible provided 'Sir' or 'Madam' is interposed at appropriate intervals. For example, in a plea in mitigation to a bench of lay magistrates it would be perfectly appropriate to proceed as follows:

> 'Madam, there are three matters relating to the defendant's involvement in these offences that I would like to draw to the attention of you and your colleagues. First, madam, there are two specific aspects of the pre-sentence report which I would like to refer you to …'

High Court and circuit judges pose more of a problem. As a general rule, 'you' should be substituted by 'Your Lordship(s)', 'Your Ladyship(s)' or 'Your Honour(s)' as the case may be. For example, in the Crown Court before a circuit judge, the previous address would begin:

> 'May it please Your Honour, there are three matters relating to the defendant's involvement in these offences that I would respectfully draw to Your Honour's attention. First, Your Honour, if I might be permitted to draw Your Honour's attention to two specific aspects of the pre-sentence report …'

To those who are unfamiliar with courtroom protocol, this version may sound unnecessarily obsequious. Nevertheless, this is the level of courtesy expected and you depart from it at your peril. The odd 'you' or 'your' here and there may be acceptable, but do not take risks until you are experienced and know your court.

12.3.4 How to refer to your opponent

It is equally important to extend all the appropriate courtesies to your opposing advocates. Choose from 'My friend' or 'The prosecution/defence' or 'Mr/Ms/Mrs/Miss Smith'. The term 'My learned friend' is traditionally reserved for barristers, although this is no longer a hard and fast rule. If you are opening the case you should always ascertain the name of your opponent since it is a normal courtesy to introduce them to the court. For example: 'Sir, my name is Mr Jones and I appear to prosecute this case and my friend Ms Smith appears on behalf of the defendant'.

12.3.5 Three golden rules when addressing the court

As well as knowing how to behave in court, an advocate must be able to create an impression of being experienced. Failure to observe the following will tend to reveal precisely the opposite.

(1) Do not give evidence yourself

Not only is this improper, it also suggests over-involvement in the client's case. Avoid phrases such as, 'My client tells me …' or 'I happen to know that …'. However, it will often be necessary to put the client's views to the court, for example in a civil chambers application or a plea in mitigation in a criminal case. In chambers applications, the phrases, 'I am instructed that', and 'my instructions are', are perfectly acceptable, but in criminal cases they are sometimes interpreted as being coded messages that the advocate does not believe a word the client is saying. Phrases such as, 'I have discussed this with my client and he wants you to know' or, 'My client wishes me to inform you,' are more appropriate.

(2) Do not give your opinion

Avoid using phrases such as, 'In my opinion …' or 'I think …'. When an advocate wishes to persuade the court to adopt his view of the case, phrases like, 'I submit,' or, 'I would seek to persuade you,' or, 'I would urge you,' are more appropriate. The important thing to remember is: the only opinion that counts is that of the court.

(3) Object rarely, but quickly

There is an enormous temptation, especially when you have thoroughly researched a case, to object at every opportunity. Indeed, this often impresses the client. However, it will not endear an advocate to the court unless the point is one of substance. Do not object unless the point advances your case or diminishes that of your opponent. Be alert: the decision to raise an objection will often be a split-second one, especially if it involves the issue of whether an inadmissible question has been put to a witness.

12.3.6 Five golden rules when questioning witnesses

Although the examination of a witness is as much an art as a science, the following are basic rules for questioning witnesses which apply whatever the nature of the proceedings.

(1) Keep your questions short

Formulate questions so that, ideally, they do not exceed ten words. If the question is convoluted there is a risk that neither the witness nor the court will be able to follow it. Nothing takes the wind out of an advocate's sails more than being asked to repeat or re-phrase a question because it is incomprehensible.

(2) Ask one question at a time

For reasons similar to those given above, it is essential to refrain from asking multiple questions. The last thing you want is for your opponent to rise to his feet and say, 'Madam, I wonder if my friend would be kind enough to indicate to the witness which question he wants him to answer first'.

This means that a quite simple point may often need to be broken down into several questions before it can effectively be put to a witness. For example, if you are seeking to extract a concession from an identification witness that she was standing 50 feet away, it was dark and it was raining, etc, you may need to ask a whole series of short questions in order to succeed in this objective.

(3) Know your objectives in respect of each witness

This applies as much to your own witnesses as to those of your opponent, but is particularly important when planning a cross-examination.

(4) Try to avoid asking questions in cross-examination to which you do not know the answer

This rule should not be taken too literally because sometimes one has no choice but to probe. The main thing is to ensure that you are never floored by the unexpected. For example, let us assume that you are cross-examining an identification witness on the issue of where she was standing at the time of the incident. If you were simply to ask 'Where were you standing?', you would have no control over the answer. Contrast:

> Q. You said earlier that you were standing on the corner of Main Street and Underwood Road, didn't you?
> A. Yes.
> Q. And there's no dispute, is there, that that is about 50 feet from the incident you say you saw?

Even if the witness says 'No', you have much more control over where to proceed from there. Alternatively, if you can easily prove that the witness was standing 50 feet away, you could quite safely ask the question 'Where were you standing?' because you know that if the witness were to reply 'About 6 feet away', you would have plenty of ammunition with which to contradict her.

(5) Know when to stop

There is always a danger in going on for too long, but it is particularly important not to fall into the trap of asking one question too many. It is a great temptation to press on when you have a witness 'on the run'. However, that is the time to pause and reflect briefly upon whether, having secured some favourable concession, it might not be wiser to refrain from cross-examining further.

For example, if you have managed to extract from the identification witness referred to above concessions that she was standing 50 feet away, it was dark and it was raining, it is a great temptation to then say with a final flourish: 'So how can you be so sure it was the accused that you saw?'.

This is the one question you (and your client) may live to regret!

12.3.7 Witnesses: court formalities

There are a number of matters of court protocol concerning witnesses of which you need to be aware, especially since it will be your task to explain them to your client and other witnesses before they give evidence.

Criminal cases

In a criminal case, witnesses other than the defendant should be asked to stay out of court until called.

If the defendant is to give evidence, he must be called before other defence witnesses.

Witnesses may refresh their memories from their written statements prior to being called to give evidence. Other parties must be informed if this has taken place.

Civil cases

In a civil case, witnesses may sit in court throughout the hearing. If the advocate wishes to exclude witnesses from court, he must apply for an order to that effect.

The claimant and defendant are both usually called first by their advocate.

Witnesses may refresh their memories from their written statements prior to being called to give evidence. Other parties must be informed if this has taken place.

12.4 OPENING THE CASE

This section considers opening speeches in all types of proceedings. Although the length and purpose of such speeches may vary widely, they are all vitally important. They provide the advocate with an opportunity to make the first impression. This can be vital, as the court or tribunal may know little or nothing about the case they are about to try. For example, in a criminal trial before magistrates, the bench will probably know nothing about the case other than details of the charges.

12.4.1 Criminal trials in the magistrates' court

The prosecution always has the right to make an opening speech before calling its evidence. In simple trials, this right is sometimes waived. If the prosecutor does open, he will usually:

(1) introduce himself and his opponent to the court;
(2) take the bench briefly through the charges;
(3) outline the facts of the case and the evidence that he intends to adduce in order to prove the charges; and
(4) explain the law, where necessary.

The opening speech requires the advocate to be a good storyteller so that the relevant incidents are brought to life. If there is an item of evidence for which admissibility is in dispute, the prosecutor should make no mention of it when opening, leaving admissibility to be determined at a later stage.

Defence advocates rarely make an opening speech before calling their evidence, because by doing so they lose the right to make a closing speech. Since the prosecutor has no right to a closing speech, the defence advocate will usually take advantage of having the last word.

Apart from the right to make speeches, either advocate may at any stage make a submission on a point of law. In particular, the defence may submit that there is no case to answer at the close of the prosecution case. In such an event, the opposing advocate always has a right to reply.

12.4.2 Civil trials

The claimant's advocate has the right to open (unless, unusually, the burden of proof of all issues lies on the defendant). As judges now have power to dispense with opening speeches, their use may decline, but the practice of handing in a written 'skeleton argument' to the judge in lieu of an opening speech is likely to increase. As in criminal cases in the magistrates' court, if the defendant's advocate elects to make an opening speech, he is not entitled to make a closing speech except with leave of the court.

The purposes of the advocate's opening speech in a civil trial will be to:

(1)   introduce himself and his opponent to the court;
(2)   indicate the nature of his claim, for example: 'Your Honour, this is a claim for damages for breach of contract';
(3)   summarise the areas of dispute between the parties;
(4)   outline by reference to the statements of case the alleged facts of the case (nothing which cannot be proved should be asserted), indicating areas of dispute;
(5)   introduce the evidence, including any matters contained in agreed documents;
(6)   summarise the legal principles involved, indicating areas where a ruling will have to be made.

12.5 EXAMINATION-IN-CHIEF

Examination-in-chief is in many respects more difficult than cross-examination because an advocate should always be seeking to succeed on the strengths of his own case rather than the weaknesses of his opponent's. Accordingly, the way your own witnesses give their evidence has a vital bearing on the overall impression that your case creates in the mind of the court.

12.5.1 The characteristics of examination-in-chief

Although, with one exception, advocates have a complete discretion as to the order in which witnesses are called, it is usual in civil cases for the claimant or defendant, as appropriate, to be called first. In criminal cases, the prosecutor will usually call the victim first, but the defence advocate is obliged to call the defendant before other witnesses as to fact unless the court directs otherwise (Police and Criminal Evidence Act 1984, s 79). The advocate calling the witness will, as a matter of courtesy, begin by announcing each witness in turn, for example, 'Your Honour, I now call the claimant, Margaret Brown'.

The principal objectives of examination-in-chief are:

(1) to present the witness's evidence in a logical sequence (usually chronological or by topic);
(2) to cover all the relevant issues upon which the witness is able to testify; and
(3) to anticipate matters likely to be raised in cross-examination.

The major characteristic of examination-in-chief (and what makes it so difficult for the advocate) is that the witness must, so far as possible, be left to tell his own story with minimal prompting from the advocate. In order to achieve this objective, leading questions are not generally permitted, neither will the witness normally be allowed to refer to any previous written statement made by him (unless it qualifies as a contemporaneous note).

Although there is a degree of controversy over what constitutes a leading question, the generally accepted definition is that it is a question which suggests its own answer by seeking to put words into the witness's mouth. For example, if an advocate was seeking to establish that a witness saw the defendant, James Smith, in The Mitre public house at midday on Monday, 21 August (all of which is in dispute), it would not be permissible to ask: 'Did you see James Smith in The Mitre public house at midday on Monday, 21 August?'

Instead, the advocate would need to proceed by means of a number of non-leading questions as follows:

> Q. Can you remember what you were doing on Monday, 21 August? (This question is arguably leading, but probably not objectionable.)
> A. Well, let me see. Oh yes, I went into work in the usual way.
> Q. Did you stay there all day? (Non-leading)
> A. No, I went out for an early lunch.
> Q. About what time was that? (Non-leading)
> A. Oh, about ten to twelve I think.
> Q. And where did you go? (Non-leading)
> A. A pub called The Mitre.
> Q. Did you see anyone there you recognised? (Non-leading)
> A. Yes, I saw James Smith …

and so on. As can be readily appreciated this technique requires the advocate to prepare very carefully in advance to ensure that he is able to guide the witness through his evidence without resorting to prompting.

The technique also requires stamina, since it may take time even to elicit a simple set of facts in this way. The only three occasions on which leading questions are permitted by way of exception are:

(1) when the witness's evidence relates to a matter that is not in dispute;
(2) where a denial is invited from the witness; and
(3) on those rare occasions when a witness is declared to be hostile.

An example of exception (1) above would arise if the only dispute was as to the date on which the witness saw James Smith:

> Q. Do you recall an occasion when you saw James Smith in The Mitre public house? (Leading, but not disputed)
> A. Yes.

Q. And can you remember when that was? (Non-leading)
A. Yes, it was on Monday, 21 August.

The advocate should always check in advance with his opponent as to what matters can be led to the witness. Matters such as name, address and occupation may always be led, but some advocates prefer to ask witnesses to state these details in their own words to help put them at their ease.

An example of exception (2) would be if Mr Smith's advocate was seeking to extract a denial from his client. It would then be permissible to proceed as follows:

Q. Mr Smith, were you in The Mitre on Monday, 21 August at midday? (leading)
A. No, I was not.

Exception (3), namely the hostile witness, is rarely encountered. It is considered in outline only.

12.5.2 The witness who does not come up to proof

Criminal cases

If the witness displays an unwillingness to tell the truth at the instance of the party calling him, the court may declare the witness to be hostile. This allows the advocate who has called him to ask leading questions and, with leave, any previous inconsistent statement made by the witness may be put to him. Such a statement may be used only to discredit the witness's testimony: it is not independently admissible. Further discussion of this difficult technique is not appropriate at this stage.

In most cases, however, the witness's failure to say what the advocate is hoping for is the result of forgetfulness, incompetent examination-in-chief or a poorly taken statement. In such a situation, witnesses cannot be cross-examined. The advocate can only try to repair the damage by calling additional evidence which supports his case. The problem of the forgetful witness may also be avoided if a contemporaneous note of his earlier evidence is available (see **12.5.4**).

Civil cases

The position of the hostile witness in civil cases is broadly similar to that in criminal cases, with one major exception: the court can be invited to treat any previous inconsistent statement as admissible evidence in its own right and, if appropriate, prefer it to the witness's oral evidence (Civil Evidence Act 1968, s 3).

If the witness is not declared hostile, the advocate's options are limited in the same way as in criminal cases (but see **12.5.4**).

12.5.3 Exchange of witness statements

The exchange of witness statements in civil proceedings has made a fundamental difference to examination-in-chief. If a party has served a witness statement and wishes to rely at trial on that witness's evidence, the party must call that witness to give oral evidence unless the court orders to the contrary. The witness's statement will stand as his evidence-in-chief unless the court orders otherwise. This means, in cases involving exchange of witness statements, that examination-in-chief has been reduced to:

(1) formally calling the witness and establishing his name and address;
(2) asking the witness to identify his statement; and
(3) asking the witness whether the contents of the statement are true.

12.5.4 Introducing documents and real evidence

Documentary evidence may be introduced for a variety of reasons. The term 'document' includes items such as photographs, tape-recordings, video films and computer data. From an evidential point of view, it is important to remember not only that a document's authenticity must be established but also that its contents must be admissible for the purpose for which they are tendered. The rules differ materially in criminal and civil proceedings.

Criminal cases

A witness must normally be called to prove the authenticity of any document which is to be adduced in evidence. Although documents cannot be agreed (contrast the position in civil cases), in practice many documents, such as agreed plans of traffic accidents, are routinely admitted. Copies of the documents are generally sufficient (see Criminal Justice Act 1988, s 27). A police officer will normally be called to prove the authenticity of a defendant's written confession. This will be done by asking the officer to identify the defendant's signature and recount the circumstances in which the statement was made. If accepted, the original will be admitted as an exhibit. The police officer will then normally be invited to read the defendant's written confession to the court. Although most interviews with suspects are now tape-recorded, the written summary of the interview will basically be proved in the same way.

The other commonly encountered document is the 'contemporaneous note'. The basic rule is that a witness may, with leave of the court, refresh his memory in the witness box from any document which was made or verified by him substantially contemporaneously with the events to which he testifies.

Police officers, in particular, will frequently ask for leave to refresh their memories from notes contained in their pocket books, but other witnesses may also be permitted to refer to their original statements.

The advocate conducting the examination-in-chief will question the witness in order to establish whether the document falls within the rules. The opposing advocate may then cross-examine the witness solely on that issue. Only after leave has been granted will any further evidence-in-chief be given by the witness. The opposing advocate is entitled to inspect the document and may cross-examine the witness about its contents, subject to certain technical rules which are outside the scope of this chapter. Although witnesses are not otherwise allowed to refer to their written statements in the witness box, the court does have a discretion to allow a witness to leave the witness box to read his statement (*R v Da Silva* [1990] 1 All ER 29). When the witness resumes giving evidence, it must be given orally without further reference to the statement.

Real evidence consisting of other objects, for example a weapon, must likewise be proved by a witness who can show that they are what they purport to be and that they are relevant to the issues. It will also be necessary to prove that an appropriate chain exists which links the object to the defendant.

Civil cases

In theory, a witness must be called on to prove the authenticity and originality of each document which is to be adduced in evidence. However, in civil cases, documents are almost invariably agreed. They will usually be put in as one or more agreed bundles by the claimant's advocate in the course of his opening speech. Furthermore, the use of documents is inextricably bound up with the rules as to disclosure, expert evidence and exchange of witness statements, all of which are outside the scope of this chapter.

The rules relating to the use of contemporaneous notes to refresh the memory and the court's discretion to allow the witness to leave the witness box to read his statement are the same as in criminal cases. These rules have effectively been overridden in cases where there are exchanged witness statements.

12.6 CROSS-EXAMINATION

Effective cross-examination is generally regarded as representing the highest level of advocacy. The skilled advocate, by harrying his opponent's witnesses with probing questions, can effectively demolish the other side's case. However, it is an art hedged with misconceptions, most of which derive from watching too many fictional courtroom dramas. The aggressive language and sarcastic manner that are characteristic of the television soap opera are usually inappropriate in the real world.

Cross-examination is a vast topic which deserves a book to itself (many such books have been written over the years). It is also a skill which requires constant practice. The basic principles can be stated fairly briefly, but detailed examination is outside the scope of this chapter.

12.6.1 Defining objectives

Advocates should always give careful thought to what they hope to achieve by cross-examination. In order to do this effectively, it will be necessary to develop a 'theory' of the client's case. This theory should be a plausible version of the events, consistent with the available evidence and the client's instructions which, if accepted, will result in the court finding in the client's favour. Once the advocate has developed this theory, he will find it easier to work out his tactics.

Another point to be borne in mind is that, whatever tactics are to be adopted, the cross-examining advocate must always 'put his case' to his opponent's witnesses. In other words, the advocate must confront his opponent's witnesses with all aspects of the client's case which conflict with their evidence. This need not be done directly. One often hears advocates saying, 'I put it to you that …' as if it were an essential ritualistic device. However, it is possible to be more subtle than this. For example, using the illustration in **12.5**, if Mr Smith's advocate needed to put to the witness that it was in fact on 22 August that he saw his client in The Mitre, it would be permissible, but inadvisable, simply to state: 'I put it to you that you are mistaken, it was on 22 not 21 August that you saw Mr Smith in The Mitre, wasn't it?'

If the answer were to be 'No', that would be the end of the matter.

Suppose, however, that the cross-examining advocate knew that the witness regularly went to The Mitre at that time: the client's case could be expressed more effectively in the following way:

Q. It's true, isn't it, that you regularly go to The Mitre for lunch?
A. Yes.
Q. At about the same time each day?
A. Yes.
Q. Around midday?
A. Yes.

The cross-examiner could continue by trying to establish that there was nothing special about 21 August, before suggesting to the witness that he had in fact got the day wrong and that he had seen the defendant on a different day.

In other respects, the cross-examiner has considerable freedom of manoeuvre in deciding how to structure his cross-examination. There are four main questions to consider.

(1) Should I cross-examine at all?

It may well be that unless the advocate needs to put the client's case, it is better to ask no questions at all. This is especially so if a witness has not directly damaged the case. Cross-examination may increase the risk of eliciting unfavourable material that would otherwise not come out.

(2) Are there any favourable matters that I can extract?

It is far better for an advocate to get a witness on his side, than to confront him. For example, in a case involving disputed identification, try gently to elicit concessions from the witness that it was, for example, dark and raining at the time, rather than suggest aggressively that his evidence is worthless.

(3) Is there any way in which I can discredit the witness's evidence?

Witnesses can, and often do, make mistakes or erroneous assumptions that can be exposed by cross-examination. Very few witnesses deliberately give false evidence. This always needs to be borne in mind when probing for weaknesses. Again, an indirect rather than a confrontational approach is likely to yield better results. Exposing inconsistencies by reference to a previous inconsistent statement is a particularly effective method. It is governed by special legal rules which are outside the scope of this chapter.

(4) Is there any way in which I can discredit the witness himself?

It is rare for the advocate to find himself in a position to insinuate, for example, that the witness is biased. It is a particularly risky tactic when done on behalf of a defendant in a criminal trial because of the dangers of falling foul of Criminal Evidence Act 1898, s 1(3)(ii). In any case, the tactic should never be adopted unless there is independent evidence available to substantiate the allegations.

The above four questions are not mutually exclusive: a cross-examining advocate may wish to adopt those parts of a witness's testimony which favour his client whilst challenging other parts which do not. This is a highly skilled and complex operation.

12.6.2 The technique of cross-examination

The major difference between examination-in-chief and cross-examination is that the advocate cross-examining is permitted to ask leading questions. This is a particularly valuable right since it enables him to retain tighter control of the witness than is the case with non-leading questions. However, leading questions should not be used to excess since this may give the impression that the witness is being brow-beaten. The tactic can, however, be particularly effective when an advocate wishes to expose inconsistencies or illogicalities. The trap can be set by asking the witness a series of non-leading questions on peripheral matters as a preliminary to confronting him with weaknesses or inconsistencies in his testimony by means of a series of tightly controlled leading questions. This is a highly skilled exercise.

Two general examples will suffice. Suppose that you were trying to discredit the testimony of an identification witness. There would no doubt be a number of matters which you had thoroughly researched beforehand, such as where he was standing, how far away he was from the incident, the time of day, the weather conditions, etc. You would no doubt wish to keep tight control of this part of your cross-examination by means of leading questions. However, it might also be appropriate to probe into what the witness had been doing beforehand by means of non-leading questions. For example, you might ask: 'Now Mr Smith, you say you were on your way home when you witnessed this incident; where were you coming from?'.

The answer might be: 'I'd been down The Mitre for a drink'.

Not all cross-examinations will yield such promising results, but it can be seen that much useful information can be gleaned from peripheral matters by means of non-leading questions without running any risk to one's case.

A second example might be in the case of a witness whom an advocate wished to confront with a previous inconsistent statement. It might be appropriate to begin by inducing him by means of non-leading questions to embellish his story still further before confronting him with his inconsistencies. This is a particularly effective technique where the allegation is that the witness is biased.

12.7 RE-EXAMINATION

Once cross-examination is completed, the advocate who called the witness has the right to re-examine. That right is limited in that: first, he may deal only with matters raised in cross-examination; and secondly, leading questions are not permitted. Very few advocates are skilled re-examiners. It is a sophisticated art. As a general rule, it is most unwise to re-examine unless you are absolutely certain as to your objectives. Its principal function is to repair any damage done in cross-examination, by giving the witness an opportunity to explain or qualify his previous answers. It is useful where, for example:

(1) cross-examination has confused the witness;
(2) the cross-examiner has attempted to impeach the witness's credit;
(3) the cross-examiner has elicited only partial details of an incident which appears to favour the opponent's case.

12.8 CLOSING THE CASE

Closing a case can be more difficult than opening, because a greater degree of improvisation is required. An opening speech can be worked out in detail beforehand: by the time an advocate rises to make a closing address, all the evidence will be before the court and the case may look very different by then. However, it is rare that the central issues will have changed, only the details. It is absolutely vital, therefore, to have identified the likely issues and evolved a 'theory' of the case in advance. It is only in this way that a closing address can deal with all the outstanding issues in a coherent and persuasive manner. It is important to remember that, just as the advocate who opens the case has the advantage of the first word, so the closing speaker is the last advocate the court will hear before retiring to consider its verdict.

12.8.1 Who closes the case?

Criminal cases

The basic rule in magistrates' court trials is that only the defence will make a closing speech. The only exception is in those rare cases where the defence has both opted to make an opening speech before calling its evidence and been given leave to make a closing speech. In such a case, the prosecution is also permitted to make a closing speech, but the defence will still address the court last.

Civil cases

Except where the defendant began or where the defendant calls no evidence, the advocate for the claimant has the last word in a civil case. If the judge says that he does not wish to hear a closing speech, then the claimant has probably already won.

12.8.2 The purpose of the closing speech

Criminal cases

Be brief. Magistrates' courts are very busy places and you will be well advised to confine yourself to the essential points which advance your client's case. However, the experienced advocate will not allow himself to be rushed. If you need a few moments to compose yourself and go over your notes, do not hesitate to ask for them. You should always cover:

(1)   any relevant points of law;
(2)   the key issues in dispute;
(3)   any part of the evidence which weakens the prosecution case and strengthens that of the defence.

Avoid saying too much about the burden and standard of proof. Magistrates need little reminding of this. It is better to concentrate on those parts of the evidence which genuinely raise a reasonable doubt.

Civil cases

The position in civil cases is broadly similar to that in criminal cases, except that an advocate must always be aware that he is addressing a judge, not magistrates. Modify your style accordingly. Since civil trials still take place on the statements of case, a closing speech which follows the issues raised by the statements of case will greatly assist the court. Judges are particularly grateful to advocates who not only summarise the issues that are still outstanding but also emphasise the essential findings of fact which the judge will have to make in order to decide the case.

12.9 ETHICAL ISSUES

An advocate's reputation with the court is his most valuable asset. An advocate who has lost the court's trust through some piece of unethical conduct is a liability. All advocates should be familiar with the Law Society's Code for Advocacy (see *The Guide to the Professional Conduct of Solicitors* (The Law Society, 1999), p 385).

12.9.1 Criminal cases

Duties of the prosecution advocate

The duties of the prosecution advocate are:

(1) to ensure that all relevant facts and law are before the court;
(2) to make available to the defence any evidence which is inconsistent with the evidence which a prosecution witness gives at the trial.

Duties of the defence advocate

The duties of the defence advocate are:

(1) to say on a client's behalf all that the client would properly say for himself;
(2) to keep confidential all information received about a client and his affairs which the client wishes to keep confidential;
(3) to ensure that the prosecution discharges the onus placed upon it to prove the guilt of the accused. The defence advocate is entitled to put the prosecution to proof even if the defendant has admitted his guilt;
(4) to disclose to the prosecution and to the court all relevant cases and statutory provisions relating to the case, even if unfavourable to the defence. However, unfavourable evidence need not be disclosed;
(5) not to participate in a positive deception of the court. A solicitor may not continue to act for a client who misleads the court (eg by giving a false name, or giving evidence which the advocate knows to be untrue) unless the client is prepared to reveal the truth;
(6) not to act for two or more clients whose interests are in conflict, even if invited to do so by the court.

12.9.2 Civil cases

Advocates for the claimant and the defendant are bound by the same rules which are:

(1) to ensure that all relevant facts and law are before the court;
(2) to say on a client's behalf all that the client would say properly for himself;
(3) to keep confidential all information received about a client and his affairs which the client wishes to keep confidential;
(4) where relevant, to ensure that the opponent discharges the onus placed upon him by the burden of proof;
(5) to disclose to the court all relevant cases and statutory provisions relevant to the case, even if not favourable to the client. The advocate may then seek to show that decisions which are against him are erroneous, not binding, per incuriam, or

distinguishable. As in criminal cases, the theory is that unfavourable evidence need not be disclosed. However, the rules as to disclosure and exchange of witness statements are such that, in practice, both parties may be required to disclose such evidence;

(6) not to participate in a positive deception of the court. A solicitor may not continue to act for a client who misleads the court (eg by giving evidence which the advocate knows to be untrue) unless the client is now prepared to reveal the truth;

(7) not to act for two or more clients whose interests are in conflict.

12.10 CRIMINAL CASES: BAIL AND MITIGATION

A detailed study of criminal advocacy in bail applications and pleas in mitigation is outside the scope of this chapter. However, a very basic guide to the skills required is set out below. Because most criminal advocates will begin their careers with a simple bail application or plea, it is often erroneously assumed that this is 'easy' advocacy. Nothing could be further from the truth: there is nothing easy about a situation in which the client may face a period in custody if his advocate fails him.

12.10.1 Bail

The skills of the advocate will be required only when the application is opposed. Although bail is always ultimately a matter for the court, it will normally be granted as a matter of course unless the prosecution objects. Since defendants have a right to bail prior to conviction, it is customary for the Crown Prosecutor to begin by formally setting out his objections by reference to the prescribed criteria in Bail Act 1976, Sch 1, Pt I. The objections will almost invariably be based on an assertion that there are substantial grounds for believing that the defendant will either abscond and/or commit further offences while he is on bail. The risk of the defendant interfering with witnesses is also frequently advanced as an objection.

The task of the defence advocate is twofold. First, he should seek to put forward arguments which tend to minimise the risks adverted by the Crown Prosecutor. Thus, for example, if the prosecution claims that there is a substantial risk of the defendant absconding, this might be rebutted by arguing that:

(1) the defendant is pleading not guilty and the evidence against him is weak;
(2) the defendant's record (if he has one) reveals that he has never absconded whilst on bail in the past;
(3) even if he is convicted, the likelihood of a custodial sentence is remote.

These are very general illustrations: each case must be dealt with on its own facts. Whatever the facts, thorough preparation is always essential.

Secondly, the advocate must neutralise any substantial risks by putting forward a sensible package of conditions, such as a surety combined with a condition of residence, which will be sufficient to persuade the bench that they can afford to take a risk and grant bail. Although Bail Act 1976, s 4 is supposed to secure a right to bail, in reality if a prosecutor raises substantial grounds for withholding bail the defence advocate has a difficult task upholding that right. An effective application, therefore, requires as much advance preparation as the circumstances permit. The Crown Prosecution Service (CPS) should always be approached (in advance if practicable) in order to obtain as much information as possible about both the offence and the defendant.

If possible, you should obtain detailed instructions from the client concerning his personal circumstances and the existence of any potential sureties. It may be that this will avoid a contested application altogether. If you can produce an appropriate package of conditions to the CPS before the hearing, you may be able to persuade them to withdraw their objections. So far as the actual application itself is concerned, an advocate should always bear three things in mind.

(1) Structure the application in such a way that each prosecution objection is countered in a logical sequence, and conclude with any package of conditions you wish to put forward.

(2) Keep the application as short as circumstances permit and remember that courts usually have a long list of cases to hear.

(3) Tailor the application to the individual client. Magistrates are often offered the same platitudes whatever the nature of the application such as: 'My client strenuously denies the charge, has a fixed address and instructs me that he has been offered work on a building site'.

The statement may be true, but it is vitally important to interest the court in your client's personal circumstances. It might therefore be more appropriate to explain a little more about why your client's denial is so significant. For example:

'Sir, if I might begin by referring you to the case against Mr Smith, you will see that it is tenuous in the extreme. The evidence consists solely of hotly disputed identification evidence ...'

and so on.

12.10.2 Pleas in mitigation

As with bail applications, advance preparation is essential. Courts can sentence only on the basis of information and, although the sentencing court may have a written pre-sentence report (PSR) available (this is mandatory when the court is considering a custodial sentence or certain types of community penalty), there will often be a great deal of further relevant background information which the defence advocate can put before the court. The Powers of Criminal Courts (Sentencing) Act 2000 places the seriousness of the offence at the forefront of the matters to which the court must have regard when passing sentence. Nevertheless, the court is not precluded from considering the circumstances of the individual offender by way of mitigation. A useful starting-point in the magistrates' court is to consult the Magistrates' Association Sentencing Guidelines.

The following eight points should always be considered when preparing a plea.

(1) Thoroughly research the realistic sentencing options available, referring, where appropriate, to relevant statutory or judicial guidelines.

(2) Take as full a written statement as possible from the client, dealing with the circumstances both of the offence and of the client.

(3) Obtain an up-to-date copy of the client's criminal record, and deal thoroughly with the circumstances of any offences which the court may regard as being 'aggravating'.

(4) If a PSR has been ordered, try to contact the Probation Service in advance of the case to see if they will discuss its contents informally.

(5) Arrive at court in plenty of time so that you can discuss your mitigation speech with the client and obtain his approval of your proposed course.

(6) When called upon to address the court, invite them to read any PSR first.

(7) When the court has read the PSR, begin your speech by dealing with matters which affect the seriousness of the offence. Then go on to deal with matters of offender mitigation, referring where appropriate to the PSR. Never read paragraphs of the PSR aloud, because the document is confidential. Instead, invite the court to consider the appropriate paragraph. For example: 'Madam, you will recall that Mr Smith's family history is dealt with at the top of page 2 of the pre-sentence report. I would particularly draw your attention to the matters dealt with in paragraph 3 ...', and so on.

(8) Conclude by 'showing the court the way home'. In other words, if you can suggest a realistic sentencing option which the court can take, you are not only discharging your duty to the client, but also assisting the court. Sentencing an offender is never easy, and anything which helps the court discharge this onerous duty will be gratefully received.

12.11 CIVIL CASES: CHAMBERS APPLICATIONS

12.11.1 Key characteristics

It is particularly important to master the skills relevant to chambers advocacy in civil cases, because trainee solicitors have full rights of audience. A chambers application is any application made to the court after the proceedings have been commenced and before the trial of the action. In the High Court, those chambers applications requiring a hearing will be dealt with by a master (in the central office in London) or a district judge (in the district registry). In the county court, these will be dealt with by a district judge. All chambers applications, whether in the High Court or the county court, share a number of common features.

(1) There are no 'live' witnesses. With rare exceptions, all the evidence will be in witness statement form. Hence the principal tasks of the advocate are to present his case and to argue for the order sought.

(2) Advocates are seated (except for some applications before a master).

(3) The proceedings are heard in public (unless the court otherwise directs).

12.11.2 Preparing for the application

Although the subject-matter of an application may vary considerably from case to case, there are a number of steps which should always be taken.

(1) Try to agree as much as possible in advance.

(2) Make sure all relevant witness statements are served before the hearing. Although the court may be prepared to accept a late witness statement, it will result in your client being penalised in costs.

(3) Make sure that you have mastered the facts of the case and that you are familiar with the contents of the statements of case and witness statements. You may find it useful to prepare a written chronology of the case including the key events and steps in the action from issue of proceedings to date. It is not uncommon for the master or district judge to deal only with those particular points in the case which he considers need arguing. Your grasp of the facts and documentation therefore needs to be such that you can locate them instantly. If

the case is a complex one consider handing to the master or district judge a written chronology which you have agreed with your opponent.

(4) The master or district judge should have a copy of the court file. However, you will need to ensure that you have copies of any relevant documents to hand to the master or district judge, should the court file be incomplete.

(5) Prepare brief notes. Although you should never read out your submissions, it will help you to have a list which sets out the points that you intend to raise. Focus on the main facts to be addressed. You might use a highlighter pen on copy documents (not the originals) for this purpose. Write in the margin of a copy witness statement a brief summary of what each paragraph contains. An example of such a note in a contract case might be: 'Para 3 – Summarises the dispute as to time of delivery'.

(6) Make sure you have read and flagged the relevant passages in the Civil Procedure Rules 1998 and Practice Directions.

(7) Have a very clear idea of the order you want the master or district judge to make. If you are making the application, you should attach to the application notice a draft of the order you propose (except in the most simple applications).

(8) Work out in advance any relevant interest calculation and costs order the master or district judge is likely to make. Also consider whether the master or district judge should make any directions for the future conduct of the action.

(9) Consider the prospect of an appeal should your application be unsuccessful. An application for permission to appeal may be made to the master or district judge at the end of the hearing.

12.11.3 Conducting the application

Whether the claimant or the defendant is the applicant, the party whose application it is will begin. The order of speaking will be the same whether the proceedings are in the High Court or the county court.

The applicant's case

If you are representing the applicant, the procedure is as follows.

(1) FORMALLY INTRODUCE YOURSELF AND YOUR OPPONENT AND IDENTIFY ANY RELEVANT DOCUMENT ON THE COURT FILE TO WHICH YOU INTEND TO REFER

For example:

> 'Good morning, sir, my name is Mr Holtam and I am from Collaws. I represent the claimant, David Mills. Miss Gibson, from Evans and Co, represents the defendant, Christopher Marlow.
>
> The claimant's application today is for summary judgment.'

You should then check that the district judge has all the documents you intend to refer to on the court file and ask if he has read them.

The master or district judge will not have copies of the correspondence between the parties or their solicitors. You should refer to such correspondence only if it is exhibited to a witness statement.

(2) BY REFERENCE TO THE DOCUMENTS, CONCISELY IDENTIFY THE ISSUES (LEGAL AND FACTUAL) FOR THE COURT TO DECIDE AND HIGHLIGHT THE RELEVANT FACTS

State the issues clearly before taking the master or district judge through the documents. Argue for the order sought on the basis of the issues you have identified from the documents.

Take the master or district judge through the documents at a sufficiently slow pace to enable him to digest their contents. It is not normally necessary to read them out verbatim; you should merely refer to paragraphs and summarise their effect. If the master or district judge has read the papers, your summary can be quite concise. More detail is needed where the papers have not been read. Refer to any exhibits in a way which ties them in with and explains the contents of the relevant witness statement. You do not need to refer to matters that are not in dispute between the parties.

If your opponent is present, you should have asked him before the hearing whether he wishes to take the court through his witness statement himself or whether he is happy for you to do this.

Anticipate and deal with all disputed matters revealed by your opponent's evidence.

(3) SUCCINCTLY REFER TO THE RELEVANT LAW AND/OR PROCEDURE

Explain simply which Rule you are relying on and apply it to the facts of the case.

(4) CONCLUDE SUBMISSIONS FOR THE ORDER SOUGHT

Emphasise what you consider to be your best points and explain briefly why you are entitled to the order sought. Be prepared to address the court on an alternative or 'second best' order if you think the court is not prepared to grant the order you really want.

If you are applying for summary judgment on a specified claim, the master or district judge will expect an interest calculation.

Make it clear to the master or district judge that you have finished your application. For example: 'Sir, unless I can help you further, that concludes my application'.

The respondent's case

The respondent's case will be structured differently as the court will by now have been taken through all the evidence. None the less, the respondent's case follows a similar model.

(1) SO FAR AS NECESSARY, IDENTIFY ANY RELEVANT DOCUMENT ON THE COURT FILE TO WHICH YOU INTEND TO REFER

The applicant should have introduced you and therefore there is no need for you to introduce yourself again. If the applicant failed to introduce you, then you should introduce yourself.

You should identify the documents that you will be relying on as a basis for your response, for example:

> 'Sir, in opposing this application I will be relying on the Defence and the Defendant's witness statement.'

(2) BY REFERENCE TO THE DOCUMENTS, CONCISELY IDENTIFY AND DEAL WITH ISSUES (LEGAL AND FACTUAL) FOR THE COURT TO DECIDE, HIGHLIGHT RELEVANT FACTS AND ADDRESS APPLICANT'S SUBMISSIONS

You should identify what you want the court to do and why.

The applicant has already taken the master or district judge through the statements of case and the evidence. Take the master or district judge to the relevant paragraphs in the statements of case and the witness statements which support your arguments. Present a positive case in support of your opposition to the order sought by the applicant. Do not just reply to the points made by the applicant. After presenting your positive case, deal with each of the applicant's points, however difficult it is to do so. Stress the effects of making the order on the action and, if it be the case, that the application is an attempt to blur the real issues and/or to prevent them being properly decided by the court after hearing oral evidence.

(3) SUCCINCTLY COUNTER THE APPLICANT'S ARGUMENTS ON THE RELEVANT LAW AND/OR PROCEDURE

Reply to the legal points raised by the applicant. Distinguish, if possible, the applicant's authorities and introduce any you rely on.

(4) CONCLUDE SUBMISSIONS AGAINST THE ORDER SOUGHT

Briefly emphasise why the order requested by the applicant should not be made (or at least, if it is made, why it should only be in modified form).

Make it clear to the master or district judge that you have finished your opposition. For example: 'Sir, unless I can assist you further, those are the grounds upon which I oppose the order sought'.

The applicant's final word

The master or district judge will normally invite the applicant to respond to matters raised by the respondent.

The applicant should deal with the points made against him preferably in the same order in which they were put. This can be done very briefly if it is a point which has already been dealt with by the applicant earlier. If it is a new point, face it squarely and be quick to point to any evidence or document that supports your assertions. Encapsulate why the court should make the order you seek.

In some cases, it may be appropriate for the applicant simply to state:

> 'Sir, in my submission, my friend's arguments wholly fail to meet the case that I put before you. Accordingly, Sir, unless there are any matters that you wish me to deal with I do not propose to address you further other than to ask respectfully that you grant the order as sought.'

Closing the case

The master or district judge then gives a reasoned judgment and writes his order in note form on the court file. This indorsement forms the basis for the order subsequently drawn up.

If appropriate, the master or district judge will give directions for the further conduct of the action. Be prepared to ask for any directions which you feel are necessary.

The party who has won usually asks for costs, and the loser is given the opportunity to reply. Be prepared to make submissions on the appropriate costs order and why.

Appeals

At the end of the hearing, the master or district judge may ask the parties if they wish to appeal his decision. An application for permission to appeal may be made to the master or district judge at the hearing. Permission to appeal may be given only where the court considers that the appeal would have a real prospect of success or there is some other compelling reason why the appeal should be heard.

Effective chambers advocacy

Although the subject-matter and nature of chambers applications cover an enormous range, it is vitally important for the advocate to make his submissions as clearly and concisely as possible in order to help the court, especially since it hears so many applications during a working day.

12.12 CONCLUSION

Although this chapter could not deal in detail with the subject, it has provided an introduction to some of the salient features of the advocate's art. It should also have made clear the fact that many of the skills of the advocate can be acquired through study and observation. Remember that thorough preparation is the key: without that, no advocate can be fully effective – however fluent his oral skills may be.

12.13 FURTHER READING

Evans *Advocacy in Court* (Blackstone Press, 1995)
Napley *The Technique of Persuasion* (Sweet & Maxwell, 1991)
Monkman *The Technique of Advocacy* (Butterworths Law, 1991)
Murphy and Barnard *Evidence and Advocacy* (Blackstone Press, 1998)
The Guide to the Professional Conduct of Solicitors (The Law Society, 1999)

INDEX

References are to paragraph numbers.